Canadian Identity

major forces shaping the life of a people

Robin Mathews

STEEL RAIL

Canadian Cataloguing in Publication Data
Mathews, Robin, 1931-
   Canadian identity

   Includes index.
   ISBN 0-88791-038-6

   1. Canada–Civilization. I. Title.

FC97.M38 1988   971   C88-090362-7
F1021.M38 1988

Cover photo: Dan Maruska, Ottawa
Cover design/typography: David Berman TypoGraphics, Ottawa
Printing: Love Printing Service, Ottawa

This book has been published with the assistance of the
Canada Council and the Ontario Arts Council.

ISBN 0-88791-038-6

STEEL RAIL PUBLISHING, Ottawa

Table of Contents

CHAPTER ONE

Opening:
The Canadian
Dialectic

An old saw has it that Canadians worry more about their identity than most other peoples in the world do. Some commentators – both Canadian and non-Canadian – believe the 'Canadian fixation' is vaguely ridiculous. But our concern has deep roots and is anything but ridiculous. It has to do with our very survival beside the most powerful imperialist nation in history. Our identity is a matter of forces in tension, a matter of dialectic.

√ Canadian identity lives in a process of tension and argument, a conflict of opposites which often stalemate, often are forced to submit to compromise, but which – so far in our history – have not ended in final resolution. As a result our identity isn't as easy to pin down as we Canadians, and others, would like. In other countries, too, fundamental arguments exist. But the elements of Canada's dialectic are unique in their character and combination. They are unique, too, because the opposites are so fundamentally different the country would be finished in the minds of many Canadians if the dialectic were broken. And so Canadians express continuing concern about maintaining our identity.

At a critical time in history, the subject of identity is especially important. We need to know about ourselves – warts and all – in order to face the future without having it blow up everything that makes us worth considering as a modern community.

The identity question is no airy-fairy concern of poets and dreamers; it is about the kind of government we will have, the way we will treat our rich and our disadvantaged, the way we will look upon the rest of the world, the allies and treaties we will make, the values we will be able to claim as 'fundamentally Canadian' values.

Many Canadians believe that our identity has been shaped in some other place than Canada, and that we live by grace of a power or powers external to ourselves. For a long time, many Canadians thought of themselves as British, and they had a basis for their feeling. Canada was not only a colony of Britain, but it went through a long evolution during which it gradually removed British powers over Canadian lives. Not until the Statute of Westminster of 1931 did Canada gain the power to make foreign treaties. Appeals to the British Privy Council as the highest court of resort were ended much later. There is no doubt, moreover, that the writers of the *British North America Act* intended us to have a constitutional system – a parliamentary system – like Britain's.

Over against the argument that our identity has been defined in Britain because of our constitutional system others argue our identity is defined in the U.S.A. People on that side of the argument claim physical geography, population movement, and North American attitudes make Canadians "American." Many of them believe that the U.S., therefore, gives us our identity.

There have been, too, other people who claim that, while external forces have, indeed, figured in shaping our identity, larger forces peculiar to this people have been at work. Climate, spatial relations inside Canada, attitudes to dominating countries, the need to communicate and cooperate on this huge land mass, and a special internationalism, they claim, have forged an identity unique in the world: the Canadian identity.

Pierre Berton's fascinating book *Why We Act Like Canadians* (1982) addresses "Dear Sam," a symbolic U.S. reader. The book is pretty obviously aimed at a mainly Canadian audience. So why the "Dear Sam"? Berton appears to have worked from an unconscious recognition: Canadians are so imbued with U.S. ways of thinking the two sides of Canadians can best be reached by having a Canadian with faith in traditional values explain Canada to a mythical U.S. reader. Berton's book doesn't say that a piece of the Canadian psyche sees itself as American. But that is a fact of the Canadian dialectic. U.S. sensibility has become so insistent a part of Canadian life it has become a real part of Canadian being. That doesn't mean Canadians are half American; the part of the Canadian psyche that sees itself as American uses a very Canadian reading of what American is. That part of the psyche forms, moreover, part of a set of Canadian dialectical tensions that have been in unique formation over several hundred years.

Dialectical tension in Canadian identity began a long time ago, maybe at the time the court of France told Jacques Cartier (1534) to go find riches in the New World when he really wanted to colonize and build a community. It has surfaced most recently in the Free Trade battle. Will Canadians attach the ultimate worth of people to the anchor of profit and the ability of the individual to make profit? Or will Canadians attach the ultimate worth of people to something else: community values, social well-being at all levels, an idea of service at home and in the world, a concept of universal justice?

To the people who want to see worth attached to the anchor of profit, most of the communitarian things Canadians have done – whether protecting industries and industrial communities or establishing universal medicare – have been activities that foster mediocrity, waste, and the second-rate. Speaking to a general meeting of the Canadian Alliance for Trade and Job Opportunities on behalf of Free Trade and the removal of special Canadian protections and incentives, Donald Macdonald said: "I don't see Canada as a sort of sheltered workshop for the inefficient, the incompetent or the less capable, I see our country as one with very considerable capacity, a very considerable record of success . . . " (*Globe and Mail*, A5, Oct. 9, 1987). Mr. Macdonald doesn't say how Canada could have gained such a record if it had been a shelter for the inefficient, incompetent and incapable.

Canadians on the other side believe the mixture of public and private, protected and open has made Canadians remarkably efficient and aware. They also believe the sense of compassion in Canadian society, the so-called security nets – pensions, medicare, equalization payments in the provinces, protections that provide Canadians with a chance to express themselves and talk to each other across the broad expanse of the nation – will be lost in a wide-open competition in which only the richest and the most ruthless operators will gain control over any activity that can make profit in North America. As a Canadian Labour Congress position paper says quite bluntly: "One of the implications of free trade is that corporate decision-making in the marketplace is substituted for public decision-making in the political arena."[1]

The implications of the Canadian Labour Congress statement are simple and clear. Public decision-making in the political arena means the whole population is effective in the strategies fashioned for the running of society. If a segment of the society is suffering, then individual taxpayers, foreign interests, corporations, and government policies are all expected to contribute to the amelioration of the suffering. Government accepts the role of humanizing force for the country. If enterprise is unfairly restricted, unable to operate with effective profit and reinvestment strategies, then individual taxpayers, foreign interests, government policies, and corporations are expected to provide the climate for viable operation.

But if "corporate decision-making in the marketplace" is substituted for "public decision-making in the political arena," then the sole arbiter of the primary good becomes enterprise seeking maximization of profit. Individual taxpayers and government policies are expected to contribute to the maximization of profit in a competitive corporate world. The needs of the suffering parts of the society are not relevant to the running of the country – except as they can be addressed through private charity and privately funded benefactions. That is why the U.S.A. – dominant free enterprise country in the world today – has vastly inferior medicare, pension, regional equalization and national cultural programs to those in Canada.

The problem with the Canadian Labour Congress statement is that "corporate decision-making in the marketplace" is not really an activity separate from the political arena. It is, rather, another political ideology that must have the full support of political power in order to function. It is an ideology that declares, simply, that no one has a right to a share of the world's or the country's wealth unless he or she can, individually, compete against all others to get it. Since, in the United States, government supports that view, individual Americans usually think of government as an enemy to be resisted. In Canada, historically, government has seriously modified that view: Canadians most often think of government as a humanitarian leader at best and a serious arbitrator between humanitarian and free enterprise forces, at worst. That is one of the reasons Canadians are often described by Americans as docile, too accepting of authority, too willing to accept government dictates. Americans don't understand that in Canada the relation between individuals, community groups, the disadvantaged and Canadian government has been significantly different from that in the United States.

The conflict between a balanced communitarianism and an unleashed competitive individualism has been evident throughout Canadian history. The two sides incarnate the root dialectic in the country, and nothing gives more vivid expression to it than the identity of the people making up the sides and the rhetoric used in the Free Trade debate. The divisions are loud and clear today. But they have always been present in the country – so much so, indeed, that they have become internalized in Canadians and are part of the Canadian personality.

To begin, Canada has lived its whole existence since the arrival of the white people in the orbit of imperial powers. After the defeat of France in Canada, this country found itself in relation to two imperial powers. The United Kingdom possessed Canada as a colony. The expanding U.S.A. wanted Canada as its own. Because of the territorial aspirations of the U.S.A., the British found expedient a policy of friendship and openness to the conquered French population and the native Indian peoples. The result has been the growth and "naturalness" of bilingualism and biculturalism as well as a history of rather more generous and humane relations with the native people here than in the U.S.A.

That is a brief summary of complex relations which unfolded themselves over a long time. Canadians often take for granted today the nature of their community, rarely conscious of the differences that would have been wrought if the French had defeated the British on the Plains of Abraham, if the Russians had decided to hold Alaska and expand from it, if the Spanish had developed a significant settlement in what is now Canada. Canadians are too often unaware of the dialectic fixed in Canadian life by the final disposition of power and territories in North America.

Nonetheless, they have given the word "imperialism" resonances that are peculiarly Canadian. On the one hand, it suggests a moral quality connected to British ascendancy and values, Canada as a British dominion, development from the mother of parliaments. That sense of imperialism was quite generally held only recently and it still has positive connotations among many in this country. As British power wanes, however, its imperialism is increasingly seen as having been ridiculous, old-fashioned, and often outright evil.

That shifting sense of imperialism and 'loyalty' to an imperial power is a guide to recent shifting relations in the Canadian dialectic.

An important argument made from at least the time of Confederation onwards was that the British connection helped to hold off the power of the U.S.A. Until the Second World War, many in Canada believed the balance provided by the British Empire/Commonwealth was necessary to Canadian survival. Some worked hard, moreover, to create Empire trade, industrial, political, and military development programs to ensure not only survival, but dominance in the world for the Empire/Commonwealth nations.

What was at stake for the people involved was whether extensions of British constitutional life (Britain and the dominions beyond the seas) would shape a force to predominate in policy-making in the Western world or whether the United States would predominate. They were aware that if an association of nations that at present make up the Commonwealth wouldn't fashion policy and power in common, they would be subordinated to the United States. That is not to say imperial relations with Britain were easy, that all involved saw the possibilities, or that the United Kingdom was sympathetic to broadly based power-sharing and cooperation.

Making a statement representative of the feelings expressed by many people in the years preceding the final defeat of an idea of Empire/Commonwealth cooperation in economics, trade, and development, Lord Beaverbrook (Max Aitken), who asserts that he became a British newspaper magnate to advocate imperial integration, describes how he saw the work of Canadian Prime Minister R.B. Bennett:

> His illustrious predecessor, Sir John A. Macdonald, Conservative Prime Minister and founder of Canada, was determined to protect the Dominion from the high economic and magnetic attraction of the United States. A railway from coast to coast was necessarily the first line of defence. At a cost far exceeding the financial capacity of Canada at the close of the nineteenth century, Sir John launched and sustained the colossal project, an all-Canadian railway from coast to coast, the Canadian Pacific Railway.
>
> Bennett was confronted with the same threat by the economic and political pressure of the United States. He tried to grapple with the menace by forging an independent economic unit within the boundaries of the Empire. Bennett's noble and majestic plan was, he believed, based on Macdonald's vision. He acted with the same intention of escaping the economic attraction of the United States which would lead to political domination.[2]

When the Second World War ended the economic and military force of the British Empire in favour of U.S. domination on a global scale, the defeat of ideas favouring imperial integration was treated as inevitable and desirable. But the same people who disparage ideas of an association of Commonwealth nations under the British Empire fail to point out what Canada has given up under an increasingly bilateral alliance with the U.S. Indeed, Canada may have destroyed the possibility of building an association more diverse than the European Community in order to opt for a relation like that which Poland has with the U.S.S.R.

Out of the argument about what Canada is – and what roots the country properly has (as a basis of identity) – two fundamentally different claims have been made. On the one side is the "colony to nation," √ "evolutionary" argument about Canada's being and character. We are, that argument says, a country that acts in concert; we care about community; we bind ourselves together; we believe in compromise, organic growth, development from roots. As a result we have created a national railway, a national airlines, national broadcasting, medicare, unemployment insurance, universal education, and so on. We have, alone in North America, a genuine three-party system in which the whole population respects the Social Democratic party. We have maintained the monarchy; we have a sense of 'the crown' as above politics.

On the other side is the "anti-colonial"√ argument. Canada, in that characterization, was kept back by the British, fettered from adopting its true, North American nature. Essentially, Canadians are Americans 30 (or 50) years behind people in the U.S.A. Left alone, we would express ourselves as a people who want to be freed as entrepreneurs, who want to move into the twenty-first century. We believe that private enterprise can best serve our needs and that public enterprise has been a harbour for the weak, the incompetent, the mediocre, and the second rate.

The argument on the two sides takes many, but usually recognizable forms. People who support the first view of Canada are called, condescendingly by their opponents, old-fashioned, out-of-date, living in the past, unrealistic, hopelessly idealistic. Those on the other side are described, equally condescendingly, as sell-out, greedy, ahistorical, anarchistic, opportunistic, and continentalist.

The people on the evolutionary side are seen by themselves (and by many of their opponents) as conservative, drawn to traditional culture, attracted to large concepts that explain human existence, centralist in government, rational, and, among people on the left, inclined to sympathy for 'socialistic' public measures. The people on the other side see themselves as spontaneous, regionalist, hard-headed, unconventional, liberal, personalist, and – paradoxically – more dependent upon feelings than reason.

A spokesperson for their overall sense of North America would probably be Frederick Jackson Turner who wrote "The Significance of the Frontier in American History" in the early twentieth century. Turner was an influential U.S. historian who developed a large following. His essential claim was that the U.S.A. created a new human being through an irrational process of return to primitivism:

> The frontier is the line of the most rapid Americanization. The wilderness masters the colonist. It finds him a European in dress, industries, tools, modes of travel, and thought. It takes him from the railroad car and puts him in the birch canoe. It strips off the garments of civilization and arrays him in the hunting shirt and the moccasin. It puts him in the log cabin of the Cherokee and Iroquois and runs an Indian palisade around him. Before long he has gone to planting Indian corn and plowing with a sharp stick; he shouts the war cry and takes the scalp in orthodox Indian fashion.[3]

That passage suggests spontaneity, adaptability, self-reliance, unconventionality, irrationality. The stance is offered by Turner as essentially peace loving, self-contained, and unsophisticated. But a little noticed sentence in Turner's book *The Frontier in American History* helps fill in the implications of the "spontaneous" nature of the character created. Turner writes: "Having completed the conquest of the wilderness, and having consolidated our interests, we are beginning to consider the relations of democracy and empire."[4]

Empire/Commonwealth advocates wanted a global association in which Canada could have a position of leadership at best and of independence at least. American/continentalist advocates want a North American association in which Canada identifies itself with the U.S., sharing standard of living and values, moving, perhaps, to forms of integration, participating in "the relations of democracy and empire."

Characteristic of statements by people of that conviction is the statement by John W. Dafoe, influential publicist, writer, and editor during the years before the Second World War when U.S. power was growing in the world and British power was waning. Writing of Canada's identity, he says:

> Canada is an American country by virtue of a common ancestry with the people of the United States. When one talks about a common ancestry between Canadians and Americans, people say, "Yes, they had a common ancestry in England." But it is something closer than that. The common ancestry to which I refer occupied the American colonies prior to the Revolution. The English-speaking provinces in Canada were settled by citizens of the English colonies along the Atlantic sea-board. The generations which laid the cultural foundations of Canada and their forbears had lived in those colonies for a hundred and fifty years – four or five generations . . . .
>
> Along the Atlantic coast, cut off from people with the aristocratic point of view, they developed an indigenous American civilization, now the common inheritance of Canada and the United States.[5]

What is important about Dafoe's comment is not that it is right or wrong but that Canadians with the other view of Canadian history would take exception to almost every point Dafoe makes.

That isn't to suggest that historians shouldn't differ, for the differences among historians form the basis out of which a rich understanding of the past is woven. But because of the dialectic in Canada – the genuinely bitter division about who we are and what our future destiny will be – Canadians need to see the study of history as essential to their lives. The same is true for Canadian philosophy. Our philosophers tell us a great deal about the Canadian character, providing us with knowledge we ignore at our peril. ✓

Though not absolute or the only shape developed, a decipherable shape comes out of Canadian philosophy up to 1950.* After that, the influx of foreign philosophies carried by an enormous surge of foreign philosophers into Canadian universities makes the philosophical landscape much harder to map. The fact of the influx is, of course, a manifestation of the dialectic.

In that decade Canadian universities expanded rapidly; administrators claiming to be caught off guard often preferred to hire non-Canadians over Canadians. Canadian philosophy was nowhere taught by the new arrivals and has had to be fought into a minute place in Canadian universities. That condition is part of the dialectic because Canadians in universities and others in power are often taught to believe the country is without identity and only a (bad) copy of foreign places. They believe Canadian materials are inferior. Those who wish to research, develop, and teach Canadian materials are very often embarrassing to university administrators. They much prefer to possess people who connect to real sources of legitimate knowledge – people from outside of Canada.

Philosophers in Canada over a hundred years were primarily idealists. They were, that is, people who believed, in one way or another, that reality consists in or depends upon minds or ideas. In essence that means they believed the real is

*The central work on the history of Canadian philosophy is Leslie Armour and Elizabeth Trott, *The Faces of Reason, An Essay on Philosophy and Culture in English Canada 1850-1950*, Wilfred Laurier University Press, 1981.

not, ultimately, the material or external world. That suggests a division between "body" and "spirit" which most people are familiar with from Christianity.

Marxism, for instance, is a materialist philosophy. Combining dialectical and historical materialism, it believes that everything we need to know can be discovered in the conflict of material forces through time. It almost goes without saying, therefore, that Canadian philosophers were rarely sympathetic to Marxist beliefs. By the same token, Canadian philosophy has contained strong criticism of capitalist materialism, present in Canada but most powerfully and significantly manifested in the U.S.A.

Capitalist materialism in the U.S.A. is often rhetorically Christian (idealist), while in practice its values are wholly materialist in a crude way. Perhaps the simplest way to explain the difficulty is to point to the fact of U.S. Christian evangelist enterprises which grow fantastically rich as a function of preaching – with every capitalist marketing technique – the Christian message of humility and poverty. Indeed, the rejection of full-scale free enterprise economics and full-scale socialist economics for a mixed economy in Canada is an historic demonstration of the struggle to synthesis in the day-to-day conduct of Canadian life.

Idealism in Canada very early underwent modification because of Canadian circumstances. Refined squabbles about the character of God and spirit imported from Europe lost credibility here. The relation of human beings to nature in Canada was close, and the intimacy invited Canadians to respect the natural world. Finally, evolutionary ideas became very strong in the Western world, Canadians adapting Darwinism to their own growing view of reality. It hardly needs saying that the identity of a people has to be tied to its explanations of reality.

Canadian philosophy has recognized the dialectic and has attempted to assert a truth that reality is made up of a relation between opposites. The opposities dramatically visible today are a balanced communitarianism and an unleashed competitive individualism. But the dialectical forces have raged for Canadians in the last 150 years in terms of the opposites of faith and reason (especially the battle between faith and Darwinist ideas), between the ideal and the material, the individual and the community, human kind and nature, Protestantism and Catholicism. The dialectic has been present, in a sense, in each Canadian.

What Canadian idealists did was to attempt to dissolve the "subject-object dichotomy" conventionally accepted by Western philosophy. Much is made of the subject-object dichotomy in philosophy. Put simply it is a question about the relation of the self to everything that is outside the self. They defined each individual as separate from but definitively a part of the community.

As Canadian philosopher John Clark Murray (1836-1917) wrote of the relation between the individual and society:

> the two are in reality one and the same principle looked at from opposite points of view. The freedom of the individual is an empty abstraction apart from the social order by which it is maintained, and the social order is properly the realization of individual freedom.[6]

In a rough and ready way, if the individual and the object (the external world, the other) are perceived to be separate, then the subject very easily becomes the "individual." In the rhetoric of U.S. usage, the "sanctity of the individual" stands in opposition to the other, to society, the state, even to his or her neighbour – as we see by the American fondness for private weaponry and law suits.

In the context of the Canadian dialectic, a decision to make a Free Trade treaty with the United States is a decision to give dominance to the American/continentalist/individualist side of the Canadian argument. It is a regionalist argument for a number of reasons. First, concepts of U.S. individualism are regionalist by their very nature. If the centre of meaning is the self and not the larger community, then legitimacy is claimed for the increasingly smaller social unit. A two-part pressure is created by the U.S. social order. One pressure is for the local, the regional, the personal, the individual to be recognized as ultimate in value. The other pressure is to expand the self, the individual to a larger and larger condition. The United States becomes a "self," an "individual State" – which, incidentally, accounts partly for the intense nationalism and patriotism of Americans which very often Canadians find strange and repugnant.

The "self" of the United States is essentially in philosophical opposition to other "selves" in the world. A Free Trade treaty with Canada is not a violation of the localism, regionalism, and individualism of the U.S. It is an expansion of the self; it is the creation of Fortress North America; it is the fulfillment of U.S. Manifest Destiny to be "self" filling the whole continent. That is not a desire to "dissolve the subject-object dichotomy." It is a desire to make the subject paramount. It is in Frederick Jackson Turner's terms to forge empire. Remember he wrote: "Having completed the conquest of the wilderness, and having consolidated our interests, we are beginning to consider the relation of democracy and empire."

Canada is a Confederation, developing its self-definition over time. Clearly, many Canadians were drawn to the prospects of evolutionary theory in constitutional, social, and political terms. A significant kind of philosophy emanating from Scotland, principally, mirrored those terms and articulates the depth of the communitarian tradition in Canada. It met the needs of a society that lived close to nature, that required the harmonizing of polarities, and that needed a concept of God which embraced harsh terms of existence as well as the beauties of ultimate Reality. Many Canadians were drawn in their considerations and modifications of that philosophy to evolutionary ideas, just as they were in specifically religious thought and action.

After the 1850s evolutionary ideas shook the whole Western world and shattered the faith of many. Simply put, Darwinism means an evolutionary, interrelated process of the development of creatures against, say, chance development or sudden inexplicable manifestations of structures and forms. Canadians thought deeply about the implications of Darwinism and argued over them much more than they did over Marxian ideas and, later, Freudian ideas.

Three major interpretations of Darwinism became current: mechanistic, individualistic, and altruistic. Mechanistic Darwinism assumes that creatures evolved from first cell to human kind, and occupy places and roles set on a fixed scale. The mechanistic view doesn't assume a Creator nor suggest much hope for beneficial change in the world.

Individualistic Darwinism led to what we call Social Darwinism. It held that creatures evolved by natural selection or the "survival of the fittest." Those unable to deal with their environment became extinct. Social Darwinists applied this theory to the social world. The poor person is, naturally, where he or she should be on the scale. The rich person is demonstrably "fittest" and deserves to survive. Social Darwinism was used through the last half of the nineteenth century into the twentieth century and is used today to claim that divisions of wealth, health, freedom, and education among people are "natural" and should not be tampered with. The U.S.A. has found Social Darwinism much more appealing as an explanation of life than Canada has.

Both views have had, however, strong expression in Canada. Indeed, the argument among pure Free Traders that "a level playing field" in North America is necessary for just, free, and unimpeded trade is, at base, an argument out of Social Darwinism. In short, they hold that if individuals and enterprises are allowed to compete "freely," the fittest (the most efficient, most productive) will survive and, finally, dominate on the continent and perhaps in the world – for, it is said with the naivete of Adam Smith, the benefit of all human kind.

Altruistic Darwinism was the most influential form to take hold in Canada. It maintains that creatures have evolved through natural selection, but that evolution is purposive, always in process, and, therefore, moving towards a better and ultimately perfected condition. The Canadians who developed concepts of Altruistic Darwinism believed in an organic relation between the poor and rich, a general striving for betterment, a goal commonly shared, and an interdependence among all creatures – manifested in a desire to ensure the well-being of others.

While Altruistic Darwinists may not have been the visible instrument of policy in Canada, their ideas were harmonious with great national projects, with the development of social benefits and securities for all Canadians, with the creation of the CCF/NDP and the wings of both other major parties which actively worked for "altruistic" political policies. Altruistic Darwinism was perhaps the most sympathetic to the view that a conventional Christian God could still be a Creator in a world seen in Darwinian terms of natural selection and survival of the fittest. The interrelation, then, of Church people and so-called 'progressive movements' in Canada makes good sense, even to the extent – as unbelief grew powerful in the twentieth century – of Church people exchanging religion for forms of stated or unstated Altruistic Darwinism.

The dialectic in Canada and developments out of the dialectic reveal an insistent force of interrelation among political decision-making, social policy, religious faith, the erection of public institutions, concepts of public service, philosophical ideas of human meaning, and description of the individual's relation to the community.

By definition a dialectical condition means the constant

movement of ideas and forces. It is not unreasonable, then, as observed near the beginning of this chapter, that Canadians are said to worry more about their identity than other people and to feel vaguely uncomfortable being unable to describe something certain and fixed.

But dialectic is our condition of life, like it or not. Being a country that has been a part of imperial systems from the first moment when white people set foot on the land, Canadians have had to make terms with powers that have always pressed upon our sense of community. The influence of imperialism upon the dialectic has been formative. People of the first empire, Catholic and Francophone, exist in tension with people of the second empire, Protestant and Anglophone. Quite apart from cultural and linguistic differences, the people of the first empire became a conquered people, adding the layer of conquerer/conquered to the dialectic. A further complication has expressed itself since the time the British realized they had to fashion policies to pacify and befriend the conquered Francophones and the native peoples in case of war with the U.S.A. The dialectic, endlessly complicated, between the ideas (real and imagined) of the U.S.A. and the ideas (real and imagined) of the United Kingdom, became part of the gift of imperialism to Canada. So, too, did the concern Canadians are said to have about identity.

That concern manifests itself in our daily lives, at all levels. If philosophers search in a theoretical world for truth as well as for an explanation of reality and a key to virtuous living, political parties also take hold of an explanation of reality and set to work shaping a society. In Canada political parties have adopted explanations of reality to stand by. But history and the dialectic have buffeted their beliefs and principles. In almost every case the story of the party is the story of its attempt to survive in the face of the contending opposites of the dialectic, and, usually, the story has not been a pretty or a flattering one.

CHAPTER TWO

The Conservative Vision

John A. Macdonald, Canada's first Prime Minister and an important architect of Confederation, was a Conservative. How he saw Canada and what he did on behalf of the nation are important for understanding the development of Canadian Conservatism, but so is an understanding of how Macdonald's Conservatism has been modified by the tension in the Canadian dialectic. Conservatism has been under constant attack as a political philosophy and, in our day, it has finally begun to crack into fragments and to be replaced by a philosophy of materialist individualism. Whether the communitarian side of the dialectical argument has been damaged irreparably is a question time alone can answer. We now live amid a "new Conservatism" which is, in fact, a distinctly different political philosophy from traditional Conservatism, one that has rushed in to fill the vacuum left by a retreating and untenable set of beliefs. John A. Macdonald's Conservatism is more notable for its difference from contemporary Canadian Conservatism than for its continuity with an older tradition.

Seen in large historic context, Conservatism is a philosophy which, properly speaking, was shaped in an epoch almost wholly foreign to our times. The dawning of Conservative philosophy – whether it was called that or not – is wrapped away in the Middle Ages, if not in a time before. It fitted feudalism well.

Conservative philosophy, over a number of centuries, developed a structure of belief that is often called organic. That simply means that its adherents saw human society in a divine order, related upwards towards heaven and God, downwards towards the inferior creatures. Human kind was a mixture of nature and spirit that transcended nature. The spirit that transcended nature could unite with God, while the portion connected to nature related human beings to the rest of physical creation. But the separation of matter and spirit was real – so real, indeed, that the postulate was used in various forms of theory to institutionalize the subjection of women, the conquest of nature, the activity of slavery.

Elaborated in social terms, a hierarchy existed, a chain of being: God, the holy angels, the monarch, the princes of the realm and of the Church, and so on down the scale. *Place* in the social order meant *meaning* in the social order. In theory, the monarch owed duties to the lowest peasant, who, in turn, owed duties to the monarch, since both were in a divinely constructed order.

When Shakespeare wrote in *Troilus and Cressida* (Act 1, scene iii) that the order of hierarchy or degree was an essential of society, he described a genuine part of Conservative philosophy:

> How could communities,
> Degrees in schools and brotherhoods in cities,
> Peaceful commerce from dividable shores,
> The primogenitive and due of birth,
> Prerogative of age, crowns, sceptres, laurels,
> But by degree, stand in authentic place?
> Take but degree away, untune that string,
> And, hark, what discord follows! each thing meets

In mere oppugnancy: the bounded waters
Should lift their bosoms higher than the shores,
And make sop of all this solid globe:
Strength should be lord of imbecility,
And the rude son should strike his father dead:
Force should be right; or rather, right and wrong,
Between whose endless jar justice resides,
Should lose their names, and so should justice, too.
Then everything includes itself in power,
Power into will, will into appetite;
And appetite, an universal wolf,
So doubly seconded with will and power,
Must make perforce an universal prey,
And last eat up itself.

Elaborated in economic and political terms, the aristocracy was the source of worldly power, land was the source of wealth. But the Church involved itself in both power and land, and so the sacred and the profane mixed every day. Production was closely related to land, agriculture, animal husbandry, and small industry. Though guilds and associations of artisans developed, sometimes growing rich, they didn't significantly challenge the structure of the order, until the advent of capitalism, Liberalism, and the new vision of classes.

When Edmund Burke wrote his *Reflections on the French Revolution* (1790) in a brilliant, ordered prose, saying that there are times when revolutions are necessary, but *this* was not one of the times, he was a King Canute standing on the shore of history ordering the tide not to come in. A Whig (Liberal) in most of his political life, Burke is now considered to have formulated a major articulation of Conservative philosophy for modern times. Perhaps that is a point worth pausing over.

Political philosophies do not hold hard and fast to particular policies through history, and as events shape the interests of nations and classes, parties shift and change. In

Canada, for instance, the Liberal Party has traditionally been the continentalist, "free trade" party. In 1911 the Liberal Party was defeated in a general election in which it advocated moves towards "Reciprocity," what we now call Free Trade. In the 1980s, the advocate of Free Trade has been the Conservative Party – an *apparent* reversal of party positions. But political philosophies – especially in so-called democratic nations – permit certain latitudes of belief. Canada, within the Western world, allows all of the possibilities that can be contained in a capitalist society: Conservatism, Liberalism, Social Democracy, and the rhetoric of strong socialism. But only by revolution could it or any of the other Western democracies set up purely socialist societies. By the same token, the Eastern bloc nations may be able to permit significant easing of centralist administration, but could not without revolution move to anything like market capitalism. When the little country of Cuba overthrew by revolution the oppressive U.S.-dominated regime, the United States was so affronted by the new socialist government that it cut off all trade, forcing Cuba into the arms of the Soviet bloc. Tensions ignited brought the world as close as it has come to nuclear war.

Canada has wider internal ideological range than the U.S.A. does. Even so, Canadians often suggest in their letters to the editor in newspapers that the United States would not "let" a New Democratic government gain power in Canada, for instance.

Edmund Burke was a King Canute because shifts in Western power and development were moving new classes and new theories of government into power, and nothing anyone could write could stem the tide of change. Conservatism could move only towards change and perhaps towards irreparable destruction of its own "fundamental" beliefs. The modern Western world doesn't believe in God – certainly not the God that informed the origins of Conservative philosophy. The modern Western world doesn't believe in a stable hierarchy – doesn't believe in a predetermined hierarchy and chain of being in human community. The modern Western world does not grant – except honorifically or by the force of economic might – hereditary power. It does not locate the source of wealth primarily in land. Production is related to land only incidentally, certainly not as a fundamental basis of economic reality.

In short, the fundamental bases of Conservative philosophy have been dislodged. God has been removed or transformed. Hierarchy has been dissolved as the stable factor in the social order. The basis of wealth – land – has been usurped by forms of capital accumulation, and production is only occasionally and incidentally connected to land. Where, then, is the basis for Conservative philosophy in the modern world?

John A. Macdonald could answer that question, as other Conservatives could for decades after Confederation because they could still locate a reading of Conservative philosophy within a viable context. John A. Macdonald's most famous statement of his Conservative belief is now almost completely misunderstood as an indication of his slavish subordination to English power: "A British subject I was born and a British subject I will die" was, in fact, an affirmation of profound political conviction at the time. It meant to John A. Macdonald's contemporaries that God was in his heaven, the monarch crowned in a religious ceremony as a continuation of governing traditions, both sacred and profane, and that an order (and hierarchy) existed in human society that gave meaning to life. While land could no longer be considered the basis of wealth, a body of belief existed which very likely included the five "dispositions" of the modern Conservative mind enumerated by U.S. theorist, Robert Schuttinger.

Modern Conservatives, Schuttinger tells us, are disposed to a belief that there is divine intent in history and that man has a duty to conform himself to God-given laws of morality.

Secondly, they are disposed to believe that order and stability are the first requirements of good government and can best be achieved by restraint and respect for tradition. Thirdly, variety, for many reasons, is more desirable than uniformity, and liberty more important than equality. Fourthly, the good life, not just life itself, is the proper goal of man. Honour and duty, therefore, take precedence over personal indulgence. Fifthly and finally in Schuttinger's list, modern Conservatives are disposed to believe that there are definite limits to the power of man's reason. Because of this, they believe a healthy skepticism should be encouraged toward abstract principles, towards intellectualism, and towards grandiose schemes for reform.[1]

In 1959, W.L. Morton, a Conservative Canadian historian set out the terms of "Canadian Conservatism Now." For Morton, Conservatism displayed the following fundamental qualities: "a respect for authority," "a similar respect for tradition," "a belief in human fallibility," "loyalty as a cardinal virtue," and "the need for continuity in human affairs."[2] Elaborating, Morton writes of the Conservative:

> He is interested in family; he instinctively wants to know who your people were and where you come from. He sees society as persons knitted by kinship and neighbourhood. And he endows society and nation with the same sense of organic life, and believes that men in particular communities are members one of another.[3]

Morton saw Canadian Conservatism, moreover, as a unique development, possessing characteristics of its own, contributed by the ultramontanism (attachment to Rome) and the ultranationalist qualities of French Catholicism in Canada, and the 'Loyalism' of the United Empire Loyalists which, while familiar with U.S. characteristics, refused "to see the king struck from the constitution, to be replaced by an elected democrat; they refused to see the legislature devour the executive and override the courts; they refused . . . to see 'all America abandoned to democracy.'"4 He pictured Canadian Conservatives in full agreement with Edmund Burke's statement that liberty could only be "the product of constitutional government." Summing up, Morton affirmed that, since John A. Macdonald,

> the essential principles of Canadian conservatism have not changed. It has remained traditional and constitutional, progressive and pragmatic. It has concerned itself with sound administration of existing laws rather than the forming of new laws, and with economic development rather than political reform.5

Morton enunciated a platform of nine points possessing a peculiar Canadian flavour. He called for recognition of the diversity of communities, the rights of the needy, the authority granted to elected representatives, a vision of universal justice, internationalism, rights to education and opportunity, encouragement of Canadian culture, a Canadian honours system, and responsibility of citizens within an elective system.

George Hogan, a long-time Conservative in Ontario – unlike Morton, a hands-on, active, Conservative party man – tried in 1963 to articulate Conservative values as they arose from the experience and the traditions of the country.6 He repeated a few of the characteristics cited by Morton: human fallibility and respect for the past, but he defined a very different kind of Conservatism from Morton's. The swing away from the past evident in Hogan's eight Conservative characteristics doesn't illustrate the differences between an academic and a Toronto businessman so much as it reveals the tension in the Canadian dialectic. It may point, also, to reasons for George Grant's passionate pessimism when he sat down to write *Lament for a Nation*.

Hogan is a serious Conservative. His book deserves attention because he is vitally aware of the world forces working on Canadians of all political convictions. But he is moving towards an articulation of values that must destroy Conservatism – in any terms in which it has existed in Canada before.

Hogan asserts God's existence. He emphasizes a search for "the best that is in [man] as an individual." He says that the "man who risks more, works more, and contributes more to society's progress, should receive a greater reward for that contribution. Conservatives," he says, "believe in political equality; they are profoundly opposed to economic levelling as an objective of political policy." He claims of the individual that the "more power he retains to himself, the more freedom he retains." Hogan says Conservatives believe that freedom is "enhanced by the private ownership of property," and that patriotism "is the highest expression of politics."[7]

Hogan's Conservatism prizes the 'risk taker' or entrepreneur, and emphasizes the good of private property. Where Morton writes of tradition, Hogan writes of heritage. Where Morton writes of loyalty, Hogan writes of patriotism.

Though Hogan has, perhaps unconsciously, moved towards principles of materialist individualism that have significant implications for the changes that are occurring in Conservative ideas of Canada, he still asserted the virtue of Canadian independence. Ironically, in relation to the Conservative position in the 1980s, Hogan wrote:

> it is one of the historic differences of emphasis between our two major parties that while the Liberals have tended to concern themselves with the symbols of our independence from Great Britain, the Conservatives have concerned themselves with the realities of our independence from the United States.[8]

And, he continued:

> The concept of an independent nation on the northern
> half of the North American continent has been a Con-
> servative ideal since colonial times. It has been upheld,
> not just by negative resistance to outside interference,
> but by positive policies designed to build upon this vast
> subcontinent a distinctive entity which one day will have
> such natural strength that vigilant policy will no longer
> be required to maintain it. Then, and then only, can we
> take our independence for granted.[9]

Hogan opts for independence, for strengthened Commonwealth ties, and for incentives to strengthen Canadian economic sovereignty, while admitting that the pressure for North
American integration is strong. Hogan's argument here is
worth examining at length since it differs fundamentally from
present Conservative policy in Canada.

> Interdependence and independence can exist together.
> In modern times, this is the relationship which I believe
> Conservatives should seek to maintain with the United
> States.
>
> The question is, do we want to go beyond this and
> work deliberately toward a larger and perhaps complete
> integration of our country with the United States? There
> is much evidence that the growing popularity of inter-
> national trade blocs is bringing about a revival of the
> old Liberal attitude of economic continentalism. For
> example, Mr. John Wintermeyer, Leader of the Liberal
> Party of Ontario, made a speech at Waterloo Ontario,
> on November 9, 1962 which was reported in the Toronto
> *Globe and Mail* as follows: *Ontario Liberal Leader John
> Wintermeyer said the province and Canada should be prepared*

for an economic union with the United States in the future . . .

"An economic union doesn't mean a political union, as this would never come about," he said. "However, we must face the possibility of a strong economic union and be prepared for it.

An economic trading pattern is bringing the two countries together, and this pattern set today will increase in the future," he said.

He said the provincial government should plan for union, so that Ontario industry is not left out in the cold when it comes about.

It is not clear what Mr. Wintermeyer means by an economic union with the United States. But if he has in mind anything comparable to the European Common Market, his suggestion that this will not mean a political union is frighteningly naive. Even the Europeans admit that their economic union has political objectives. But it at least is a union of countries of relatively comparable size and power. For the independence that each member surrenders to that union it gets in return a measure of influence over the whole undertaking which provides some protection for its own interests. But in a bilateral economic union between two such unequal powers as Canada and the United States we could not expect to exert anything approaching equal influence. Such an arrangement is not a union, but an annexation.[10]

George Hogan left the question of a Canadian and Conservative future hanging in the balance. George Grant, a major Canadian Conservative intellectual, did not. In his now famous book, *Lament for a Nation* (1965), he declared that the "impossibility of conservatism is the impossibility of Canada." In his view, the values of Conservatism upon which Canada was founded were being ground out of existence as Liberalism, representing the policy of big corporations and the philosophy of technological society, was sweeping over and homogenizing all North America.

⌐Grant claimed that Canada's founding was wholly a function of the communitarian side of the dialectic. Of course it wasn't: annexationists were active in Montreal in 1854, and John A. Macdonald had to surrender his concept of a unitary state for a "confederation" of states. Moreover, even before Confederation, the country was founded as a major activity of entrepreneurial exploitation of native peoples and resources, planting a firm root of liberal capitalist development that did not evaporate in the debates preceding Confederation.

Because George Grant refused to see the country's founding in dialectical terms, he projected the defeat of traditional Conservatism in his day as the destruction of Canada. Certainly, the Conservatism Grant valued is no more.

The shift began, for Grant, with the English philosophers Thomas Hobbes, John Locke, David Hume, and Adam Smith, whom Grant saw as the philosophers of capitalism; he calls them, too, the philosophers of greed. In an article entitled "Theology and History," he settled on an examination of the Will. When human Will operates within a belief system, he argues, it is directed and controlled by values in a structure usually much larger than the self. When such systems break down, the Will, in a sense, is let loose. In a statement heavy with implication, Grant says that "the English-speaking elites are fast becoming Nietzschean."[11]

The implications are enormous because Nietzsche rejected the Christian structure of beliefs and he stated that a fundamental of human psychology is the will to power; intrinsic in that is the will to brute power. The struggle of the individual will is to achieve the state of the Ubermensch or Overman, which we have come to translate as the Superman. For Nietzsche, the Ubermensch is not guided by a divine power nor does it find itself in a communal structure of values, but it is almost a self-creation in a world without purpose, part of a cycle of directionless activity that will go on and on . . . .

The implications of George Grant's statement, then, begin to come clear. Nietzsche not only rejected the concept of a Christian God, he also declared that Christianity is a gathering of the weak, the failures, people who deserve to be oppressed. Though philosophers argue about the seriousness of some of Nietzsche's cryptic statements, an idea easily distinguishable in his thought is that reason and restraint are negative values, opposed to the truth found in the passionate, the anti-intellectual, the body.

The state of Nazi Germany is said to have been influenced by that interpretation of Nietzschean thought. But Grant was primarily concerned with the Nietzschean position in its relation to liberalism and the advent of technology. In short, Grant believed our concept of justice was shifting from one based on the innate worth of human beings to one based on the need to operate a technocratic system effectively. The Nietzschean argument focusses on the individual, rejecting communitarian and traditional definitions of human dignity. It locates significance where power is centred. In a fragmented liberal capitalism, power is located at the centre of the technocratic system and, in Nietzschean terms, is solely responsible for declaring what is good and just.

That claim puts Grant squarely in the centre of the fundamental Canadian dialectic; and it connects him with other major Canadian thinkers and writers. He continues the tradition of thought developed in Charles Norris Cochrane's *Christianity and Classical Culture* (1940), in which Cochrane argued that the introduction of Jesus into classical ideas of justice inserted the idea of an unhalting progress into the Western world and into modern secular liberalism generally. Such an idea of progress, in turn, connects to the definition and perception of time found in the work of Harold Innis. As Innis reminds us in *The Bias of Communication* (1951) the annihilation of time is the annihilation of culture. Technology, number, and capitalist money are the prime annihilators of time in any traditional, communal sense of the word 'time.'

Innis spent most of his adult career writing about Canadian economic history and, towards the end of his career, about communications and empire. His ideas are at once mainstream and trail-blazing in Canadian thought. He was intensely aware of the dialectic and its relation to Canadian (and world) survival. His illegitimate intellectual son was Marshall McLuhan, mass media and television guru. Innis was among the communitarians, the seekers of means to anchor values in human worth. Obviously influenced by Innis and declaring his indebtedness, McLuhan was among the individualists, the technologists, the seekers of an anchor of values in the cash nexus – for him described in the reality of U.S. power. McLuhan's famous 'global village,' as critics are increasingly observing, was electronically connected to the big tent (the U.S.A.) where all major signals are intended to originate.

McLuhan was the illegitimate intellectual son of Harold Innis because he took ideas, technical theories, and the huge global scope of view Innis developed in a highly moral and peculiarly Canadian perspective, de-natured them of their moral character, and attempted to erase any relevance that Canadian being had to the structures of thought Innis built. The two very modern men provide a Janus mask. They manifest the dialectic, facing two ways, apparently adopting the same body of material as a basis from which to work.

The argument implicit in the difference between the two men needs explanation because it is a key concept. In simplest terms technology, number, and capitalist money are said to homogenize economic and cultural activity. Language, on the other hand, is said to define and reinforce culture and tradition. Number breaks down culture and tradition. Language is culture-laden; number is culturally neutral. As number and the technology that depends on the use of number become more powerful than language as a social force, the uniqueness of cultures and societies is threatened. Capitalist money is a form of neutral number in the marketplace. We hear many expressions like "the dollar has no boundaries," "money has no country," and "time is money" – statements that suggest unique cultures impede the movement of capital or are irrelevant to it. If those statements are true, then 'time' – as tradition, as a present depending upon a past, as a manifestation of customs formed through generations – is annihilated by technology, number, and capitalist money.

Capitalist money, in these terms, is not just a means of exchange. It is, rather, a self-producing value whose primary reason for existence is to multiply, and to remove or efface anything that obstructs its most efficient multiplication. A culture-laden concept seems to be coming into conflict with a neutral or 'universal' one that is unconnected to culture. But any neutrality is only apparent. Just as, in Chapter One, the phrase "corporate decision-making in the marketplace" seemed to be a non-political opposite to "public decision-making in the political arena" but was, rather, a concept depending on redirection of political priorities, so the annihilators of time do not stand outside the culture. They stand, in fact, for a revolution in the culture; they represent a culture of the *now,* a culture perhaps best described by Nietzsche, one in which the ultimate liberal individual engages in self-creation in a world without purpose – within a cycle of directionless activity that goes on and on . . . .

George Grant, then, perceived the death of Conservative philosophy in Canada and lamented the forthcoming demise of the Canadian nation. Within Grant's terms, developments in Conservatism since 1965 confirm his position. A young 'traditionalist' Conservative in Brian Mulroney's office told me about his own presence at a Conservative Party think-tank meeting in Toronto in the early 1980s. Major invited speakers, he said, were individualist, free enterprise, monetarist representatives from Britain and the United States, lauding individualist, cash-nexus values. Finally, Robert Stanfield, a former leader of the Conservative Party, addressed the meeting, reminding it of traditional Conservative philosophy in Canada – not primarily individualist and cash-nexus oriented. One person, the young man telling me the story, leapt to his feet at the end of the speech to lead the standing ovation, but not another person in the audience rose to join him.

In terms of traditional Canadian Conservative philosophy the Conservative Party of the 1980s is a major departure. It is individualistic, materialistic, pro-U.S., continental integrationist, anti-traditional, and anti-communitarian. The Quebecois are quite right to call it the "new Liberalism." Conservatism may swing back at some time in the future, for unless the Canadian dialectic is destroyed, possibilities will remain open. But now, Conservatism in Canada has joined the U.S. side of the dialectic.

The new Conservatism practises *revisionism* in the truest sense of the word. A revisionist (a word usually used in relation to Left politics) is someone who changes the root basis of a political philosophy by changing the meaning of words key to the articulation of the philosophy. When confronted, revisionists insist the original words have always meant the most recent definition given to them. A contemporary member of the party which calls itself Conservative might argue that the members of the Conservative Party of Canada would agree with all the characteristics of Conservatism presented in the early parts of this chapter. But that would only be true if key words in the definitions were "laundered" as to their meaning.

The alarm that we might feel after watching the movement of Conservatism over the last few decades into a redefinition that must be dangerous for the balance of forces in Canada may, perhaps, be mitigated by a consciousness of how the dialectic has always been at play here, and the capacity Canada has to re-form apparently fixed loyalties and partisanships to assure that, whatever else passes, the dialectic survives.

CHAPTER THREE
The Liberal Vision

The Liberal view of society has predominated in the Western world for at least two hundred years. It has dominated the writing of history in Canada, and has shaped the very air Canadians breathe. There is an extent to which all Canadians are, in some sense, Liberal, because they live in a Liberal ✓ Capitalist Democracy. That fact pulls Conservatism toward Liberal belief, modifying Conservatism in the process. The power position of Liberal belief also pulls Left political belief towards it, modifying socialist and other leftward political philosophy in the process.

Because of the ubiquity of Liberal ideas, Liberal thought, Liberal environment, most Canadians couldn't define Liberalism if asked, and many Canadians who think they have no politics and belong to no political party express Liberal ideas when asked what their personal, self-constructed, wholly independent ideas and beliefs are. The most powerful ideology may do more, therefore, than modify the other political forces; it may engulf the so-called non-political elements of the society. And, finally, it may modify one or other of the political forces to the point of perverting it beyond recognition. Such is true with contemporary Canadian Conservatism. The destruction of Canadian Conservatism in our time has resulted in a free enterprise party which is, in fact, a Liberal party – but a bizarre, twisted Liberal party in Canadian terms.

Ironically, George Hogan described the condition of Canadian Conservatism gone bad when he addressed "Right-wing radicalism" and U.S. Conservatism:

> In the Conservative millenium every man is a paragon of individualist achievement, so Conservatives should be against the welfare state; in the Conservative millenium political power is diffused in wide and classic balance, so Conservatives should be against federal aid programs; in the Conservative millenium, the Russian Revolution would never have occurred, so Conservatives should keep trying to undo that revolution.[1]

Because of the pervasiveness of Liberal ideas in Canada – as perverse as Conservatism has become – Conservatives may very well be sincere when they claim that their party has not changed.

√ Liberalism is a modern political philosophy. It came into being with the approach of the Industrial Revolution, its apologists being Thomas Hobbes, John Locke, David Hume and Adam Smith. John Locke's philosophy significantly influenced the U.S. Constitution, and Adam Smith, appropriately, published his keystone work *The Wealth of Nations* in 1776, the founding year of the U.S. nation. Whatever Smith really wrote in *The Wealth of Nations*, it has been used as a basis for many of the arguments made by modern capitalism for a preferred position in Western societies. Indeed, Smith articulated most of the ideas popular in the rhetoric of capitalism: that the state (government) and the marketplace should be separate; that commercial activities in society should be self-regulating; that enterprise left to itself will increase wealth for all members of society; and that an increase of commerce is directly related to an increase of freedom. Smith's most potent argument – one that became an abiding fundamental of Liberal philosophy – was that the pursuit of the individual's apparently ⌐ selfish interests will result in the highest collective good. If interference and participation in enterprise by government are strictly avoided, Smith allowed, and the marketplace left to respond to its own motivations and forces, an *invisible hand* will order human affairs and the ordering will be good. Smith's theory is still the fundamental article of faith behind the meaning of "free enterprise."

The overriding aspect of Liberal belief is, therefore, the economic aspect. It places capitalists in a position of primacy because it sees them as the most important people in society. We live in a Liberal Capitalist Democracy because our society believes that the individual, unimpeded in the marketplace, working successfully will, doubtless, become the wealthy person, the capitalist. That is one of the major, often unspoken, reasons our society is constructed the way it is.

Marxism, too, articulates what is essentially an economic philosophy, but with a difference which can best be seen in a simple and direct description of it written by a Canadian economist unsympathetic to Marxism and socialism. Stephen Leacock wrote:

> modern socialism came in with the machine age. It takes its departure from the ground that such things as equality, the right to vote, and free competition will not of themselves warm the body or feed the stomach. More than that, it was argued, as by Karl Marx (1818-1883), the great apostle of the socialists, that the more free the competition the more the weak are trampled by the strong. People with no property, he says, have to sell their labour power to people with property, who wouldn't

buy it unless it brought in more money than they gave for it. Seen thus, individual liberty and equality are not bread but a stone. What does it profit a man to have the right to refuse work, if refusal means starvation?

Socialism starts with the idea of all people working together, under their own joint management and sharing up the product. It is a beautiful picture.[2]

In years preceding and with the publication of *Capital*, Karl Marx established what has come to be the fundamental reply to the Liberal theorists. It is an anti-capitalist and an anti-individualist reply. Differing from traditional Conservative philosophy, both the Liberal and the Marxist philosophies (and their many subdivisions and revisions), however, are materialist. Liberalism doesn't declare itself materialist; Liberals may individually call themselves anything at all. But the fundamental philosophy of Liberalism requires no God or Eternal. It requires only the atomic individual seeking his or her own good in competition with others in society.

Liberalism was, in the beginning, a radical political and economic philosophy. The idea of placing the individual at the centre of political thought was a revolutionary one in a society seen to be marked by order, hierarchy, and "degree" as Shakespeare used the term in *Troilus and Cressida*. Trying to characterize Liberalism simply and summarily in the contemporary world, Benjamin Ward said it had three major ideals: "Affluence, openness, and welfare."[3] Its theory of the nature of man could be summed up in three words: "hedonism, rationalism, and atomism."[4]

L.T. Hobhouse, a sympathetic expositor, listed what he saw as the main elements of Liberalism. They are civil liberty – the impartial reign of law; fiscal liberty or responsible government; personal liberty – freedom of thought, speech, press, religion; social liberty – freedom of opportunity, freedom of association; economic liberty – freedom of trade, of contract; domestic liberty – equality of women, marriage as contract, defence of children; local, racial, and national liberty; international liberty; political liberty and popular sovereignty.

Liberalism, Hobhouse says, is "in every department . . . a movement fairly denoted by the name – a movement of liberation, a clearance of obstructions, an opening of channels for the flow of free spontaneous vital activity.[5]

Since Adam Smith, Liberalism has developed a war within itself. An enormous rift is always possible in Liberalism – as great a rift as seen in Conservatism at present. The rift in Liberalism focusses on the responsibility of the individual in society; the rift in Conservatism focusses on the responsibility of the community, as manifested in our day by the state.

How is it possible to speak of the "liberation" of any person, force, or idea if the liberation assures the subjection of another or other persons, forces, or ideas? That problem began to haunt Liberalism early in its life in the Western world. It meant, irresistibly, that the liberation of the individual in whatever sphere, had to be weighed in relation to the good, and to the freedom, of the rest of the community.

The liberating of the individual can have grim effects for society. Adam Smith's picture of an ideal universe gave rise to so many monstrous inhumanities that the Liberal Canadian historian A.R.M. Lower could write in 1954:

> Freedom . . . paradoxically works against "free enterprise". "Free enterprise" allows too much to the individual of superior capacities, particularly in that the capacities which enable people to "get ahead", are frequently not the most desirable: aggressiveness, a sure eye for the main chance, selfishness, inability to see much in life except power and gain, and other similar

qualities have never commanded man's highest approval.
/The virtually complete *laisser-faire* society leads to the
slave society . . . .[6]

Although Lower nowhere defined Liberalism in his book
on "the Liberal Democratic way of life," he came close to a
modern definition in his discussion of the "central problem of
our times," and it is interesting to note in the quotation below
how in Canada the dialectic within Liberalism mirrors the
abiding Canadian dialectic:

> The major problem of our times resides in the region
> just discussed: how to harmonize collectivism and free
> enterprise, control and liberty, order and freedom, sta-
> bility and adventure. If states with free institutions cannot
> solve this problem, it cannot be solved. Self-governing
> countries, by debate, will eventually square the circle
> and reconcile socialism and liberalism. They will do this
> taking one step at a time.
>
> Genuine liberalism will always range itself against
> a stifling collectivism, just as it has always in the past
> ranged itself against an exploiting free enterprise. Liber-
> alism will range itself against stifling collectivism because
> if justice means anything it must mean something to the
> individual and, under "blue-print" collectivism, the indi-
> vidual becomes a mere bit of machinery. Liberalism is
> essentially a social balance wheel, seeking the widest
> range of benefits to all, but not committing itself to any
> preconceived theory of society; at one time it is against
> unbridled individualism and at another time against
> repressive collectivism. Liberalism is a thing of the spirit.
> It is human decency.[7]

Lower romanticizes: Adam Smith's *invisible hand* is nowhere
evident in Lower's characterization of Liberalism; indeed,

George Grant's "philosophers of greed" would hardly recognize what Lower has written. But that is not for a moment to asperse Lower's view. For the nineteenth century in Europe and Canada put economic Liberalism under a magnifying glass and found it wanting. In Canada's case, the Social Gospel movement of the last quarter of the nineteenth century and first quarter of the twentieth forced new concepts before the attention of Liberalism.

The Social Gospel movement attacked the exploitative relation of capital to labour and sought remedy in Christian terms and Christian teaching. It might be called, without serious exaggeration, the father of the CCF/NDP, as we shall see in Chapter Five. But it also influenced the direction of Liberalism in Canada for the first three quarters of this century. W.L. Mackenzie King, longest governing Prime Minister of Canada was, in youth, a Social Gospeller. His book of economic/social theory, *Industry and Humanity* (1918), was a Social Gospel tract. King was hypnotized by capitalist wealth, but like other Social Gospellers he wanted to teach it good manners. He didn't want to believe in the inevitability of class conflict, for that would have meant taking sides and his humanitarian predelictions might have forced him to ally himself with the exploited and the poor. Rather, he allowed himself to be employed by the Rockefellers and helped to set up pussy-cat company unions, knowing which side his bread was buttered on, and probably believing that his activity would reduce the likelihood of class conflict.

His book placed the theory of "the Law of Blood and Death" over against the theory of "the Law of Peace and Health," attempting with those Gothic phrases to see class conflict as a universal contest of nature which all must address. Perhaps there is no greater ironic manifestation of the Canadian dialectic than a former employee of the Rockefellers becoming Prime Minister of Canada and the presiding agent in the construction of many of the social securities which we take for granted as expressions of compassion in our community life.

Liberalism has permitted itself such a wide pendulum swing in the twentieth century that the most vicious form of individualistic exploitation can be called Liberalism and so can a welfare state society providing wide employment opportunity, security in economic life, and health care from the cradle to the grave.

If Canadians seem puzzled about what parties in the country stand for, they have every right to be. Part of their puzzlement arises from the fact that the Liberal Party held power for decades by riding the Canadian dialectic. In the process, governing Liberal politicians helped to establish the sense Canadians developed that government would, as I wrote earlier, fall on the side of humanitarianism on the whole or it would at least be a serious arbiter between capitalist interests and the needs of the people. That sense of government is under traumatic assault in the 1980s.

In a piece originally written in 1959, Conservative historian W.L. Morton suggested that four developments affected political philosophy in the mid-twentieth century. The first three were the transformation of agrarian societies into industrial ones, the practical implications of scientific research, and the enormous acceleration of social change.

The fourth change Morton called "the end of philosophic individualism, or the extinction of the true liberal." He wrote of the change as it appeared on the surface. What he said, however, is most significant for its deeper implications:

> The radical survives, and the socialist, but the liberal who was an individualist, a rationalist, and an internationalist – who was also, be it acknowledged, at his best a humanitarian, and a man of generous instincts and magnanimous mind – that kind of liberal is gone with the top hat and the frock coat. The world is poorer for

his going, and it behooves conservatives to remember that they are in fact his residuary legatees, and that the liberal spirit now finds almost its sole dwelling place in conservative minds.[8]

Morton was not describing "philosophic liberalism" at all, but a romantic version of the Liberal, one perhaps most at home in a Dickens novel. Morton's quotation reveals a good-natured uncle, undoubtedly wealthy, certainly powerful, but nonetheless possessing humanity, a large view, and a generous outlook. The events in Canadian history up until 1959 when he wrote his essay obviously affected Morton's sense of Liberalism. He must have believed that the previous Liberal social welfare legislation had robbed the party of its individualistic, internationalist (in the sense of boundaryless), and rationalist (in the sense of unemotional) claims. To some extent he was right, although Adam Smith free enterprisers never completely abandoned the party – and maintained considerable influence in it. In an astute balancing act, the party adopted the position of the 'natural' ruling party because it could represent most ethnic factions as well as the whole population in a Liberal Capitalist economy.

The deeper implication of what Morton wrote is the unconscious recognition that Liberal and Conservative philosophies in Canada were in a state of transfer. Increasingly after the date of his essay, Conservatism in Britain turned to crudely free enterprise focus, attaching its political philosophy to reactionary free enterprise Republicanism in the United States. Incentive was given and pressure placed on Canadian political parties to respond. Canadian Liberalism stumbled and equivocated and set up Free Trade feelers in the Senate in charge of Liberal Senator George van Roggen by the closing years of Pierre Trudeau's prime ministership. But the Liberals couldn't or didn't want to move from what many saw as their "traditional" position in Canadian political life.

Since the time of Mackenzie King, the Liberals gave economic power to the U.S. while framing and asserting symbols of political power. By the close of Pierre Trudeau's prime ministership when – to court popular support – the Liberals attempted to repatriate some economic sovereignty, they were forced to buckle over the powers of the Foreign Investment Review Agency and to promise to make no further sovereign moves – after the National Energy Policy – towards a Canadian industrial strategy. Apart from the fact that they had to make a show of defending their own policies or proposed policies, Liberal leaders could not move towards greater continentalization because its 40-year image portrayed the Liberal Party as a party of the people, not of continental free enterprise.

The situation Liberalism had made for itself by the time of Pierre Trudeau's departure was touched with historical irony. Liberalism in Canada has generally been on the individualistic side of the Canadian dialectic and on the pro-U.S. side. In the 1890s the great supporters of U.S.-Canadian integration were the Liberals. The first major work written in favour of annexation was *Canada and the Canadian Question* published in 1891 by Goldwin Smith, a wealthy Toronto Liberal. He declared the border "unnatural" and preached the destiny of Canada as part of the U.S.A. In the twentieth century, Wilfred Laurier's Liberal government was removed from office in 1911 for advocating a "free trade" agreement with the United States. And in 1935 the defeat of the Conservative government saw the Mackenzie King Liberals reject the concept of Canada's role in the Empire-Commonwealth for a policy of U.S.-Canadian integration. In 1968 Peter Newman wrote in *The Distemper of Our Times* that the two unannounced priorities of Canadian Liberalism were individual rights and an unacknowledged policy of economic integration with the United States. George van Roggen's senatorial committee on Free Trade during the last years of Trudeau's prime ministership was a manifestation of historical Liberal policy still lurking in the background.

Trudeau himself embodied the contradictions and ironies. He was Prime Minister of the Canadian nation-state even while he professed contempt for the nation-state. He wrote that "the concept of the nation-state, which has managed to cripple civilization, has managed to solve none of the political problems it has raised, unless by virtue of its sheer absurdity . . . ."[9] That attitude and his carelessness of Canadian economic sovereignty prepared the way for preachments that Canada could not survive except by continental integration.

Gad Horowitz, also in 1968, recorded wittily that the "secret dream of the Canadian liberal is the removal of English Canada's 'imperfections' – in other words, the total assimilation of English Canada into the larger North American culture."[10]

The shifting allegiances in the two institutions which call themselves the Liberal and Progressive Conservative parties is no mystery, according to Horowitz. He pointed out that "the primary component of the ideology of business-oriented parties is liberalism . . . ." Horowitz went on to say:

> If we define ideology as a complex of ideas which is used to legitimate behaviour, we may say that Republicans have access only to the liberal ideology in legitimizing their behaviour, while British and, to a lesser extent, Canadian Conservatives have access to both liberal and tory ideologies. A Republican is always a liberal. A Conservative may be at one moment a liberal, at the next moment a tory; he is usually something of both.[11]

Horowitz's argument may have sounded more credible in 1968 than it does now. But if we consider the resiliency of the dialectic, we may be ready in a few years to see it as more convincing. The flexibility Horowitz refers to may be the result of the fact that we are a constitutional monarchy. In that sense, we are a country with many Tory/Conservative institutions existing in a genuinely Liberal Capitalist economy. Horowitz makes a useful distinction between a liberal society integrated by agreement from below and a conservative one integrated by agreement from the top in a common loyalty to the crown.

> We ought not to forget that the historic identification of toryism with the monarchy, and the antipathy or coolness of liberalism thereto, has been one of the most important distinctions between these two ideologies in Britain and on the Continent. True liberals may be able to accept hereditary monarchy, but they cannot love it. The historic anglophilia of Conservatives and the historic American-ophilia of the Liberals are also not devoid of ideological meaning. A true tory cannot be expected to adore the land of liberalism; a true liberal cannot be expected to idealize a country choked by feudal survivals.[12]

Describing the beliefs of the Conservative historian W.L. Morton, Horowitz says Morton rejected the "dangerous and improper idea of the electoral mandate." Morton believed, according to Horowitz, that ministers of the crown "ought not to see themselves as agents carrying out instructions given to them beforehand by the people, but as governors acting according to their own conception of what the common good requires. The people should not presume to *instruct* their governors, but *trust* them to govern well.[13]

As far as he goes Horowitz is right. But his book was published before the Liberal prime ministership of Pierre Trudeau, who persistently argued that he must be left alone to govern; every four or five years he claimed to be answerable to an electorate. But he was not, he claimed, an agent carrying out instructions in his task of governing.

In the push and pull of the Canadian dialectic, Liberalism and Conservatism overlap, displace each other, merge, and separate. Being subject to universal suffrage, of course, neither party can give itself openly to the support of a naked free enterprise in which the well-being of the population depends solely on the wealth of the powerful and private charity for sustenance. The general population has had to be wooed. The two free enterprise parties have their legislative life in the Parliament of Canada to which Canadians can elect others than Liberals and Conservatives. Canadians have done so, and do so. For in the sweep of modern history since the Industrial Revolution the arguments of both groups have been questioned in a way that has challenged their power and legitimacy. So compellingly has that challenge been uttered in the last 150 years that more than half of the world's population lives in systems whose governments reject the world views of Conservative philosophy and Liberal philosophy. Even in the Western world, so-called Left parties are significant forces, having won power in most of the major European countries and in several Canadian provinces. What is *their* fundamental philosophy? From what modern sources do *they* spring?

CHAPTER FOUR

The Left Vision
of Canada

The Liberal philosophy that emerged with Adam Smith, in a world increasingly untenable for the old Conservative philosophy, associated commerce with liberty, preached the separation of the marketplace and the state, and held that the wealth accumulated by the pursuit of selfish interests would sift through the population and all would benefit. But even the most unobservant person had to see an enormous contradiction developing in the Western world. The amount of wealth in the world was increasing, the wealthy were growing wealthier, trade was expanding, commerce was growing – and yet huge segments of the population were living in increasing squalor, sickness, penury, and oppression. Questions about the wisdom of Smith's theory were inevitable. As the English poet Oliver Goldsmith said, freedom of the marketplace created a population "Where wealth accumulates and men decay."

As history has shown us, the answers most powerfully and influentially delivered to the questions posed by Adam Smith and market liberalism were the ones formed by Karl

Marx, whose major work, *Capital*, was published in 1867, the year of Canadian Confederation. As has been pointed out, Adam Smith's major work, *The Wealth of Nations*, was published in the same year as the U.S. Declaration of Independence (1776). The accident of those dates is useful for an examination of the polar opposites of the fundamental dialectic in Canada.

The formulating document founding the United States – as has been observed – was based very much on the philosophy of John Locke, one of the philosophers George Grant lists among the philosophers of greed. Emerging from a complete political break with the United Kingdom, the U.S. set up a "new," "revolutionary" society based on self-reliance, competition, and self-fulfillment, in other words on individualistic "success." When immigrants with socialist ideas began landing on the U.S. shore, that country, having hardened a single Liberal philosophy, effectively effaced their ideas. A balance to free enterprise Liberal Capitalist Democracy ("the American Way of Life") was not welcome. As a result, the U.S.A. today has no significant party of the Left in its national fabric, as Gad Horowitz points out.[1]

The formulating document founding Canada was based very much on the evolutionary development of parliamentary traditions in the United Kingdom. The milieu from which the document emerged was one in which the two founding (white) cultures, Francophone and Anglophone, had to make room for each other. In the 91 years that had passed since 1776, Darwinist theories had blossomed, along with increasingly literate and concrete criticism of the philosophies (and practices) connected to the U.S. Constitution. The Industrial Revolution was significantly more advanced and its problems more universally recognized. Canada remained in constitutional relation to the United Kingdom, and did not establish its own citizenship until the middle of the twentieth century. And so when immigrants came to Canadian shores from Britain with ideas of Fabian socialism and theories developed from Marxist thinkers, those immigrants were legally and constitutionally a part of Canadian society. When immigrants came from other parts of Europe, the experience of a bicultural Canada tended to cushion their differences in a way that was unprecedented in the United States.

It would be folly to say that Left political philosophy and activity have had as unruffled a time in Canada as other political philosophies and activity have had. They have not. As one might expect, the views that arise out of Marxist theory and any serious socialist theory challenge and anger people who accept the philosophies of Liberalism and Conservatism. Canada, after all, is a Liberal Capitalist Democracy, part of a continent structured upon the beliefs of Liberal Capitalist Democracy, in a Western world almost wholly operating on a system of Liberal Capitalist Democracy. Despite a rhetoric of pluralism and claims that we possess an open society, harassment of all political philosophies and organizations critical of Liberal capitalism has been the rule rather than the exception in Canada. The fact that socialist movements and Left ideas have managed to become integrated into the mainstream of Canadian society is, therefore, a very significant manifestation of the dialectic in this country.

Fundamentally and simply, a Marxist has a materialist view of history in which the relations of production are judged to determine the kind of life lived in personal, social, and political spheres. Marxists, in the beginning, rejected idealist explanations of reality, which means they did not believe reality was in the mind or ideas but in the objective world through time. That, of course, ruled out a transcendent God, and is one of the reasons why Christian religions rejected Communism as 'godless.' Today, time having tempered social belief, many Christians and people of other faiths involve themselves in what might be called Marxism-in-the-world. That means they make use of Marxist theory and Marxist analyses of society in their day-to-day living without experiencing their belief in God and in a religious creed as a contradiction of their view of the world. When Existentialism began as a philosophy, it was atheistic. Now there are serious Christian Existentialists. When Marxism began, it was atheistic. Now there are serious Christian Marxists in the sense I have indicated: Christians who cannot think seriously about power and the ownership of the means of production in Canadian society, and elsewhere, without using analyses created and developed by Marxist thought.

It would be a mistake to suppose that the philosophical view of society Marx offered to the world over a hundred years ago is irrelevant to debate in our day. At present, more than half the world lives under governments significantly based on Marxist thought. They vary from Communist bloc governments which claim to base their existence on Marxist thought to Socialist and Social Democratic governments that hold power through democratically contested elections.

Governments of those three kinds have some very different qualities – which we will examine. But they share certain values. First, they contest, as a primary belief, the idea that unhindered capitalism creates the best society. Secondly, they question the justice and validity of bourgeois class power. Thirdly, they believe that the people, the working classes, the great mass of human kind should define the meaning of human civilization, not a class or classes who possess power through the ownership of the means of production: since all of the people make the wealth of nations, all people should share in the ownership and the benefits derived.

Canada has not had any pure Marxist governments, nor (despite commentaries by editorial writers in Canadian newspapers) has it had any Socialist governments. Canada has a Social Democratic party and it has had some Social Democratic governments in the provinces. If one were to describe key differences among the three kinds of political philosophy, one might say that pure Marxist ideas require the destruction of capitalism and the creation of a society in which a version of a peoples' government is created in a "dictatorship of the proletariat." That phrase means that history has moved to an inevitable phase in which the ideas of opposition parties and vying philosophies are obsolete.

Socialist ideas also require the destruction of capitalism and the dominance of a government that involves considerable participation from the general population. Since Socialism believes in the people as the basis of civilization, it requires in its theory that the ownership and the benefits derived from the means of production should be equally distributed throughout the population.

Both of those political philosophies have been active in Canada, with varying degrees of success and influence. The fact that they overlap in their beliefs and are often equated doesn't matter to this discussion. The distinction made here is intended to help us to think about a gradation of severity in the insistence upon the absolute necessity of throwing down capitalism and the capitalist class, the elevation of government by some form of the mass of the people in power, and the universal sharing in the ownership and the benefits derived from the exploitation of the means of production.

Social Democracy is suspicious of the claims of capitalism, but doesn't believe capitalism must be destroyed. It believes in the regulation of capitalism and the surveillance of the capitalist class. It believes in the validity and efficacy of non-capitalist enterprise (crown corporations, cooperatives, collectives, etc.). It believes, at one and the same time, in the sanctity of the individual and the rights of the larger community. Finally, Social Democracy believes that the people, the working classes, the great mass of human kind should participate significantly in the definition of civilization and should share in the benefits derived from production.

Social Democracy obviously has some of its roots in Marxist thought, but it also has roots in Christianity and in the ideas of Liberals and others who have cared for the fate of the powerless people in society. The leader of the new Democratic Party in Canada in the 1980s, Ed Broadbent, for example, wrote a Ph.D. thesis on John Stuart Mill, who is often thought of as one of the fathers of modern Liberal thought. Social Democracy has other sources of its philosophy, too. But its beliefs are a far cry from those written into the Communist Manifesto by Karl Marx in 1848, calling for a program of revolutionary reform, declaring that the bourgeoisie has brought a proletariat into existence, and that the struggle between the two is the key to modern history, the outcome of which will be the violent overthrow of the present social order.

The focus of analysis in the political philosophies we have been looking at is on the economy and the relation of the whole population to the economy. The Marxists have taught most modern social thinkers to believe that *the way* a community produces things and *the owners* of the means of production (free enterprise capitalists, government, crown corporations, collectives, or other) significantly shape social structures like law and legal systems, religions and forms of worship, class, communication systems, and artistic theories.

Political thought which is described generally as Left concentrates on the examination of power and the ambitions of capitalists, the development of the economy, and the role of the working class – focusses, it is clear, far from the history of battles, government changes, "great personalities," and even constitutional change, though all of those subjects, of course, enter a Left review of history, reconsidered from a new and often unsympathetic perspective.

Because of the nature of Liberal Capitalist Democracy in Canada as it has been presented here – jealous of its position of dominance and eager to invalidate theories critical of capitalism in Canada – full-scale Marxist treatments of Canadian history have been slow in coming. For that reason, Stanley

B. Ryerson's work, widely ignored or attacked by Liberals and Conservatives, repays examination. Ryerson wrote *The Founding of Canada*, published in 1960, and *Unequal Union* (1968). In describing the focus of his second volume, he summarized the central preoccupations of people who, from a Left perspective, have rejected Liberal and Conservative views of Canada. As Ryerson sees it, understanding class is central to understanding the history of Canada:

> Capitalist industrialization within the framework of a colonial empire; the emergence of a class of businessmen and their general acquisition of power ("Le regne des hommes d'affaires . . . etait commencé" – as LaFontaine's biographer observed); the formation of a class of wage-workers and, through their struggle with capital, the beginnings of organization, and of political consciousness: all these are elements of an evolving *class structure,* socio-economic and political.[2]

Ryerson shared a common cause with many historians and others who were not Marxist. Michel Brunet, the Quebec 'nationalist' historian, and the Montreal school of Quebec historians agreed with Ryerson that a fundamental flaw entered Canadian capitalist development when the beginnings of industrialization and reasonable self-sufficiency in Canada were cut off in Quebec by the Conquest of 1760, and strangled in English Canada by British imperial interests.

While their descriptions of history have some similarities, Ryerson and Brunet differed in their interpretation. Ryerson's argument, based on classic Marxist theory, wanted to show that capitalism in an imperialist form gutted the development of Canadian society entering its bourgeois capitalist stage, and thus prevented the next stage – the takeover of power by the working classes. Michel Brunet and other Quebec histor-ians of his conviction wished to demonstrate that English-dominated capitalism wiped out nascent French Canadian capitalism, took over social, intellectual, and economic power from the Quebecois, and rendered Quebec society 'unnatural.' For Brunet, the struggle in Quebec was not so much to achieve working-class control as to reachieve 'normalcy' for the Quebec community; to re-establish, that is, in the hands of Quebecois, power over bourgeois capitalist society.

More interesting and perhaps more important, Ryerson gives examples that prove that, long before Marx was heard of, people in Canada were discussing conflicts that produced Marx's analysis. A quotation Ryerson includes, from 1837, deals precisely with the matters that concerned Marx, who was at that date completely unknown in North America and almost unknown in Europe. The editor of *The Vindicator* wrote:

> The traders, as a body, are a useful class, but not the most patriotick. The spirit of traffick is always adverse to the spirit of liberty. We care not whom the remark pleases nor whom it offends; but it is the truth, which all history corroborates, that the mercantile community, in the aggregate, is ever impelled by sordid motives of action. The immediate interests of trade, not the permanent interests of their country, supply their strongest impulse. They peruse their ledger with more devotion than the Constitution; they regard pecuniary independence more than political; and they would be content to wear ignominious chains, so that the links were forged of gold . . . an equal currency is to them a phrase of better import than equal rights, a uniform system of exchange a grander object than a uniform system of freedom. For a sound social polity one must look to the classes whose labour is the real source of wealth.[3]

In that same year, from London in England, the London Workingmen's Association sent a message of support to the discontented workers of Lower Canada (Quebec):

It is then today or never that the working classes must strike a decisive blow for their complete emancipation . . . . A parliament which represents only capitalist property owners of money or land, will never protect the working classes; its object is to make money dear, and work cheap; yours on the other hand is to lower the cost of money and raise the price of labor; between these opposing interests peace is impossible.[4]

The force of quotations like those ones included in Ryerson's history is increased by the fact that – search as one might – neither they nor quotations of the same tenor appear in histories written by non-Marxist historians before Ryerson.

For Marxists, a view of history that accepts Canada's movement from colony to nation through the fight for responsible government to eventual sovereignty would be an idealization of the real, materialist explanation of Canada's history. They see the real history as the implanting (against all resistance) of a subordinate Canadian capitalist economy, as part of a larger imperial system.

A Marxist view of Canada accepts quite simply that capitalist interests in the imperial centre and in Canada would not want a different system to develop than one profitable to the wealthy in power. Thus the land companies, presented with millions of acres of land, both enriched their owners and created potential workers, forced to sell their labour to live. When the creation of land companies was protested, Lord Goderich argued:

Has it . . . been . . . considered . . . whether it would conduce to the real prosperity of the province, to encourage every man who can labor to do so only in his own account, to obtain and cultivate the allotment of land without giving or receiving assistance from others? Without some division of labour, without a class of persons willing to work for wages, how can society be prevented from falling into a state of almost primitive rudeness, and how are the comforts and refinements of civilized life to be preserved?[5]

At the same time, the Navigation Acts forbade shipping to or from the colonies in any but British ships; a ban on clothing manufacture in Canada was in effect; trade was restricted with the U.S. and the West Indies; and the postal service was inefficiently run from England. In 1821, the *Quebec Gazette* complained:

> The power of regulating the trade of the Colonies, which belongs to the British Parliament, is in fact a power over the fortunes, the industry, and the prosperity of every individual in the Colonies.[6]

Strictly speaking, one might think that the terms of the Canadian dialectic in political philosophy should be pure Marxism as against pure Capitalism. But that is not the case, just as the dialectic in community terms is not Canadian Capitalist democracy over against Cuban Socialist or Hungarian Communist society. The dialectic that exists in Canada in community terms is mixed economy and social security over against U.S. individualist economy and *laisser-faire* social competition.

History since Marx (and indeed before Marx) has offered systems different from pure capitalism. Many Canadians have preferred to draw from them than to work for pure Marxist solutions. A number of forces have conditioned Canadian attitudes and preferences, some positive and some negative. While U.S. distaste for any left political formulations has certainly negatively affected the life of Marxist organizations in Canada, so did the years of Moscow- and New York-centered focus in the Communist Party of Canada. A characteristic of militant Marxist organizations has been near-contempt for the national question in Canada and for the idea of serious focus on Canadian life and problems. Canadian history awaits the militant Marxist formulation that is also truly attuned to Canadian history and problems as well as to the character, style, and sensibility of average Canadians. The success of such a force can't be predicted since no precedent exists to hold up as a model.

Canadians have developed positions critical of Liberal capitalism from ideas arising out of Christianity, claims of national uniqueness, the idea of a mixed economy, a need to express tolerance between founding white peoples, and a need to provide national, unifying programs of security. On the one hand, Canadians have been aware of the claims of Marxist thinkers who have added significantly to social analysis in the country. On the other hand, they have felt a need to draw eclectically upon reform ideas in order to satisfy needs unique to the country.

Canadians who reject what might be called pure Marxist views of Canada and also reject the Liberal and Conservative views usually promulgate a vision that might be called NDP, might be called Social Democratic, might be said to sit squarely at the centre of the dialectic. That view usually accepts the capitalist system as a basis for the operation of the economy, but insists upon seeing other economic aspects as equally or more important. Writing in a key book in this regard, Herschel Hardin described the three basic contradictions in Canadian experience "(1) French Canada as against English Canada; (2) the regions against the federal centre; and (3) Canada as against the United States."[7]

Hardin discussed the complexities within Canadian society caused by those contradictions, and he attacked Canadian colonial-mindedness. But he concluded that the really definitive characteristic of the country was its economic make-up.

The more an explorer "of the colonial ideology" pursues study, Hardin said, the more "it appears that Canada, in fact, is a *public* enterprise country, and that native *private* enterprise is a somehow secondary, untrustworthy phenomenon, although it exists on a substantial scale and in most sectors of the economy."[8] Indeed, Hardin asserted "the received colonial image of Canada as a free enterprise country must therefore be upside down. The American-ideology-in-Canada, with all its phantasmagoric potency, stands Canadian reality on its head."[9]

Hardin chose, in opposition to the slumbering calmness of Liberal and Conservative reaction to threats to the survival of the country, to simplify the Canadian dialectic until the individualistic, free enterprise side was merely an aberration in Canada, a fantasy that only applied because of our colonial-minded readiness to accept outside descriptions of our country that did not in reality obtain.

But our condition isn't as simple as that. Nations in the Western world have undertaken, since Hardin wrote, "privatization" – the selling off of public enterprises – and "deregulation" – the handing over of operating standards to free enterprise organizations from governmental control. In Canada's case, both of those activities have been engaged in, threatening the public enterprise economy at all points. Canada, moreover, in a move towards what is called Free Trade with the United States, is stepping toward marketplace (free enterprise capitalist) domination of trade policies, law, political institutions, and personal welfare. Hardin's vision of Canada is one in which communitarian needs and responses to those needs have defined the Canadian nation. He argued for the dramatically central nature of the construction of the CPR, the formation of the CNR, CBC, Air Canada, Polymer Corporation, Ontario Hydro, Quebec Hydro, B.C. Hydro, equalization payments among provinces, unemployment insurance, medicare, and old age pensions. Whereas the most sympathetic Liberal and Conservative commentators have acknowledged the public enterprise aspect of Canada's economy and culture, Hardin insisted it not only provided the fundamental definition of Canada but also secured our identity. Combined with the three contradictions intrinsic to the country, our public enterprise economy, he claimed, places us in a unique position: "exactly because we were the losers of the American Revolution . . . we can now become winners of a Canadian one."[10]

Since the Second World War, views more or less like Hardin's have been the property of people connected to the CCF/NDP. They have also been taken up actively by leaders among Left Liberals who have usually lived lives of considerable tension, often suffering political destruction because of their views. The person who comes to mind most quickly in that regard is Walter Gordon, the Toronto capitalist who fathered the famous *Watkins Report* (1967) on foreign ownership in Canada, helped found and lead the Committee for an Independent Canada, and was an active, outspoken fighter against nuclear weaponry. He was, in effect, politically destroyed by the Liberal Party for his work. Eric Kierans, too, was destroyed politically because of his anti-continentalist position. Pauline Jewett discovered she belonged with the New Democratic Party after Pierre Trudeau shut her out because of her disagreement with him on Quebec and foreign policy. Mel Hurtig, Chairman of the Council of Canadians and publisher of the *Canadian Encyclopedia*, has been both rejected by the Liberal Party because of his nationalist convictions and uneasily re-embraced by the Party at various times, most recently when the Mulroney Conservatives stole the Liberal's continentalist position and strategic nationalism became a convenient way to describe a difference between the Liberals and the Conservatives.

Those names of leading Liberals who have found themselves in real conflict with the Liberal Party make clear that the position of the New Democratic Party defines a place alien to Liberal belief.

On the surface the nature of the political spectrum seems clear, but it isn't. Old Conservatism was responsible for Confederation, the CPR, the CBC, and Air Canada. The Liberals – under pressure from the CCF/NDP – were responsible for medicare, old age pensions, and U.I.C. To the old Conservatives, nation-building meant having a definable nation. To the Liberals, equality of opportunity for all meant not only the opportunity for profit-making but also the opportunity for all to live in reasonable safety, good health, and comfort. The latter is not merely a hollow statement, for Liberal W.L. Mackenzie King, longest sitting Prime Minsiter of Canada, began his life as a Christian Social Gospeller and wrote an influential book on the harmonization of capital and labour already referred to: *Industry and Humanity.* His time in politics is seen by his admirers as a period devoted, almost mystically, to riding the dialectic in Canada as a way of keeping power and keeping this Liberal Capitalist Democracy together despite regional, linguistic, and imperial pressures, and to keeping it on a compassionate path. His enemies, of course, see him quite differently.

Nonetheless, the soil out of which politicians, indeed most Canadians, of the first half of this century sprang was a soil deeply imbued with evangelical, socially responsible, class-conscious Christianity. Religion in Canada has been a significant partner in the formulation of philosophy, imperial ideas, Conservative theory, education, and in the founding and development of the most influential Left, non-Marxist forces in Canada.

Darwinism, as has already been pointed out, found itself shaped into an altruistic concept among many influential Canadians. Philosophy – the attempt to provide a basis in reason for structures of social being – in Canada found itself attempting to dissolve the subject-object dichotomy, and, in doing so, to dissolve theological dualism, with the result that the relations between classes and among creatures became an insistent question. Religion found itself in a New World wilderness that required more tolerance of the entrenched differences between Catholic and Protestant, and fostered inter-denominational openness. (Canadians rarely, for instance, note that the rhetorically "free" and pluralist U.S. did not elect a Catholic President until 184 years after the country's founding; Canada elected a Catholic Prime Minister 29 years after Confederation.) Religion in the second half of the nineteenth century found itself in the midst of what has been called, all over the Western world, the Social Question. ✔

That was the question W.L. Mackenzie King, later Prime Minister, tried to answer in *Industry and Humanity;* Salem Bland, Methodist Minister and a founder of the United Church of Canada in 1925 tried to answer in *The New Christianity* (1920); and A.E. Smith, Methodist Minister and then Communist Party activist tried to explain in *All My Life* (1949). Many others tried to answer the question in a stream of books published between the middle 1880s and 1930.

Essentially the question asked what the relation of capital and labour was, what responsibilities they shared, and what was to be the guide for humane and compassionate interaction. If not the Marxist solution of a violent overthrow of the existing order, what forces were to act to produce justice, good health, comfort, and security for all?

The Protestant churches offered a measure of leadership. In Canada the Social Gospel movement educated, propagandized, organized toward enlightened relations between labour and capital, and pressed for ameliorative legislation. Church people who engaged in the movement pushed hard for institutionalized social services and for a new recognition of the legitimacy of working people. The Winnipeg General Strike of 1919 was probably influenced by a general atmosphere created after the successful 1917 Bolshevik Revolution in Russia. But the Strike was much more affected by the disappointed promises of the First World War period, growing urbanization and industrialization, and the work of effective social reformers like Ralph Connor (C.W. Gordon), Nellie McClung, J.S. Woodsworth, Salem Bland, A.E. Smith, and William Ivens.

In a brief statement, Richard Allen, a major analyst of the Social Gospel in Canada, reveals the mixture of ideas and forces shaping reform directions over at least three decades:

> For some time the notion that Jesus and the earliest church were the first socialists had played a role in legitimizing socialism, and it was part of the creed of Marxists like Dr. J.W. Curry, a Chilliwack dentist and member of the Socialist Party of Canada in British Columbia, that the religious life of the nation would shift with the economic base.[11]

The effectiveness of the Social Gospel movement was curtailed, however, partly because of the structure of religious institutions and their connections to the capitalist class. As a result, the Communist Party of Canada was founded 12 years before the CCF – 12 important years, for the Communist Party was organized in the years leading up to the Great Depression and for four years into the Depression before the founding of the CCF in 1933. The Communist Party, founded needless to say, on Marxist principles, worked effectively in the Depression organizing the unemployed and in trade union work.

Even though it was founded after the Communist Party, the CCF grew more from the roots of the Social Question and the Social Gospel than from Marxism. Many of its founders and leaders were men who were clerics or who had left clerical life. They bore the marks of the development of ideas in Canada, and strove to find means, short of revolution, to ameliorate the lives of ordinary people and to open the doors of education, social mobility, and economic opportunity to all Canadians, regardless of class, race, or religion.

Whereas Conservative and Liberal philosophies were firmly founded in European fact and re-shaped in Canada to make the Canadian manifestations we know, Social Democracy in Canada was much more significantly forged in this place, of this place, and has felt the influence of forces outside the country upon it in a different way. The CCF was not blind to U.S. as well as British influence, and felt the force of F.D. Roosevelt's New Deal in its earliest years. The party's reformulation into the NDP gave it a name that tacked the word New to the name of one of the major U.S. parties. But for all that the CCF/NDP is a political manifestation, as pointed out, impossible in the U.S.A. The U.S. did not develop altruistic Darwinism in a significant way, or religious tolerance, or an influential Social Gospel movement, nor did it feel the political need to make a serious response to anti-capitalist criticisms or the cry for working class justice. Canada developed a party and a Social Democratic ideology peculiar to this country; the U.S.A. did not develop either.

CHAPTER FIVE

Religion in Canada: Its Effect on Canadian Identity

The outward manifestations of religious faith have waned considerably since 1957 when 60 per cent of Canadians attended churches. In 1986 Church attendance dropped to under 40 per cent. Among Catholics the drop has been most dramatic, from a high of 80 per cent in 1957 to just over 40 per cent.[1] Despite those statistics, Canadians still record themselves as believers in a large percentage, a fact which isn't surprising considering the strong force religious belief has had in Canadian history.[2]

At the present time, for instance, it is an unwise politician who will call himself or herself an atheist. Politicians may keep their faith to themselves or they may go Church-hopping as the Premier of British Columbia is said to do, especially near election time. But they may not express negative ideas about the Creator. Most Canadians believe that faith in God among their legislators is some insurance against outright evil in the conduct of public life.

Christian missionaries, we are told, accompanied rapacious traders and territorial expansionists into lands of the aboriginal peoples in order to prepare the way for commercial forces. There is enough truth in the charge and enough concern in Canada about the ugly treatment by whites – in the past and in the present – of native peoples that the role of the churches as "savers" and "civilizers" has come seriously into question in our day.

Such was not the case in the beginning. One of the founding texts of Canadian history and imaginative writing is made up of the reports of the Jesuit missionaries in Canada, produced after the first decade of the seventeenth century until near the end of the century. Gathered into 70 volumes, the Jesuit *Relations* are a testament to the Christianizing zeal of Catholicism in Canada's early history. The zeal mirrored the fact that, for more than a century and a half, Church and State in French Canada were in close union. Their bond remained close after the Conquest (1760) until at least 1960. Such an association could not but affect Protestant churches in Canada, which had to co-exist with a strong institution that stressed the authority of Church and State here, while at the same time it guarded an ultramontantist (Rome-centered) position.

Protestant 'democratic' elements affected Roman Catholicism too, helping to create an institution early involving lay representatives.[3] The Roman Catholic Church, moreover, in the nineteenth century, found itself allied with non-Anglican Protestant groups to prevent Anglicanism from becoming the Established Church in Canada as it was in England.[4] Its alliance with dissenting groups – at whatever distance – contains some irony, because by its action Catholicism described itself as a faith among the others, though it, of course, maintained its claim to be the uniquely Christian church.

Imperialism helped to create two cultures possessing the original religious dichotomy among white settlers. H.H. Walsh[5] claims John Calvin and Ignatius Loyola, Canadian 'spiritual founders,' possessed striking resemblances in their lives, their spiritual motivations, and the ways in which they constructed social responses to faith. Although there were large differences between the people influenced by the two men, similarities such as Walsh points out made coexistence easier than it would have been with frankly antagonistic versions of religious faith.

Canadians must know that differences in religion had to be tolerated in order for a Catholic, Wilfred Laurier, to follow a Protestant as Prime Minister of Canada. Genuine tolerance must also have had to exist in the community for Jewish David Lewis to succeed Christian Protestant fundamentalist Tommy Douglas as leader of the New Democratic Party. There can be no doubt that the existence of two founding cultures in Canada has had an effect on religious tolerance – for the good – no matter how many decades were spent in unreasonable alarm, suspicion, and consternation among some sects, arising from the astonishing fact (to them) that *other* (and of course) *seriously faulty* views of the Almighty had gained ineradicable place in the Canadian community. For instance, in an undated book on the Orange Order published in Eastern Canada just over a hundred years ago, the frontispiece illustration shows a man being tortured on the rack while three hooded figures look on. The caption under the illustration reads: "How Rome makes converts."

The argument over an Established (state recognized and encouraged) faith involved Canadian religious organizations in political life. Indeed, before those battles, the founding of New France was a Catholic action uniting Church and State from the start. By the same token, the United Empire Loyalists not only arrived in British North America with loyalty to the monarchy, many of them also believed the hierarchical view Anglicanism provided of a divine order. Anglicanism in nineteenth century England has been described as the Conservative Party at prayer. In Canada, United Empire Loyalism presented two faces, both with a fundamental view of political order under divine dispensation – whether in the hierarchical terms of Anglicanism or in the fundamentalist terms of Baptists and Methodists with essentially egalitarian biases.

Out of the histories of numerous Protestant religious organizations, certain clear patterns emerge. Religious organizations in Canada originated, largely, in Britain, in the U.S., or – in an often contentious rivalry – in both countries. Canadians in every case modified the identity of the imported faith to make it workable in Canadian society. Comments are common, for instance, that Scottish Presbyterianism in Canada soon dropped intense conflicts that had no relevance here, shaping an identity all its own. Such claims for Judaism are less frequent, partly because U.S. institutions trained rabbis for Canadian Jewish congregations until the late twentieth century. Nonetheless, Jewish critics have claimed that A.M. Klein, one of North America's finest Jewish poets, could only have been produced in Canada. Consciously or unconsciously, they are suggesting Canadian Jewishness has shaped an unique identity.

When conflict opened on the status of the faiths in Canada and the prospect of an Established Church – a conflict that began before the end of the eighteenth century and continued for at least 50 years – all groups found themselves forced to define the Canadian community in order to argue the reasonableness of their own relation to the community as a whole. After the War of 1812, for obvious reasons, pressure arose for independence among Christian organizations connected to U.S. bodies. John S. Moir, for instance, points out that there was no "official objection to American Methodist infiltration during the War of 1812." "Anti-American pressure was, however, felt strongly," he says, "within the Canadian Methodist body; it led to the move in 1824 by the Canadians for complete separation from the [U.S.-centered] Genessee Conference, a move completed in 1828 by the establishment of an autonomous Canadian Methodist organization."[6] Resistance to U.S. connection was very clearly not a matter only of Tory or Anglican feeling.

After the YMCA was founded, in England in 1844 and then in Canada and the United States in 1851, Canadians found themselves in serious disagreement with their U.S. brothers, especially when the Confederation of YMCAs of North America began meeting in 1854. Both the Toronto and the Montreal organizations objected strongly to U.S. racism and variously withdrew from the Confederation or attended only as observers in protest until after 1864 and the emancipation of the slaves in the U.S.[7]

Canadians rarely think about the fact that witch burnings and 'Salem trials' were not characteristic of spiritual life in Canada. The fact is significant both politically and socially. The new England settlements were up against a range of mountains that had to be crossed before population could spread. At the same time the U.S. was formed and for the next two decades church affiliation has been estimated to have dropped to something like 10 percent in the U.S. population:[8] Thomas Jefferson, whose materialist Deism may have affected U.S. religion ever after, declared specifically that the founders of the U.S. were not establishing a Christian nation. Nonetheless, the founding and early settlers in the U.S. were often intensely evangelical, intensely individualistic, intensely dogmatic Christians. The passion of their beliefs and the close proximity in which they had to live with the rest of the population – caused by life in a seaboard community – released intense conflict and zeal. By comparison, the Roman Catholic settlers of New France took for granted a Christian universe into which they fitted, even when they were railed at by members of the clergy for neglecting the faith. The bulk of the first Protestant settlers, furthermore, added to by the United Empire Loyalists, were neither as compulsively individualistic theologically as their U.S. counterparts, nor were they fenced in by mountains. The settlers in Canada were reasonably secure in their faith and, for the time, reasonably broad in their scope of tolerance.

At the time of Confederation, Canadian churches participated actively in the vision of the new nation. They were used to participating in arguments about the community and so they considered Confederation a matter of the definition of their own being. H.H. Walsh wrote that "leaders of the churches vied with one another in their support of the coalition government that had achieved Confederation; and it would seem doubtful that the administration of Sir John A. Macdonald would have survived its first appeal to the people if it had not been for the churches' intervention into the political field."[9] Egerton Ryerson, Methodist, was as active in support of the new nation as was Archbishop Baillergeon, Catholic. Battles over separate schools soon arose and continued for many decades, creating deep and lasting divisions, but the churches believed the move towards independent nationhood was imperative, whatever quarrels might develop after Confederation.

Pioneer life, vast distances, and thin population also affected Canadian religious structures. People of different churches were often neighbours who depended upon one another, invited to respect each other's humanity. Shortages of clergy resulted in common worship among people who would not otherwise have joined together in spiritual activity. The conditions of pioneer life made inherited differences and conflicts within some faiths irrelevant. And once lessons were learned from experiences of ecumenism and tolerance, people discovered compromise could be a positive and vital principle in other community relations.

There was, it is true, individualism in religion, especially on the frontier. Revivalist waves were real and powerful, and personal conversion was preached and attained in pioneer communities. But the larger element was also present: the two modes of social reform, personal salvation and community action, developed alongside one another.

The presence of the churches in Canadian politics was an established tradition by the twentieth century. The struggle between science and faith (Darwinism and Christianity) had opened Protestant Christianity especially to a new sense of the relation between classes and among all creatures. The effect was significantly different in Roman Catholic Quebec. Having by then suffered in separate schools battles, feeling itself a small island in a sea of English Protestants, and reacting to a global weakening of Roman Catholicism (which also resulted in the decision to declare Papal Infallibility in 1870) Roman Catholicism in Quebec moved towards corporatism. It moved towards, that is, a defensive, fortress mentality in which the survival of the community was to be primary, and the elements of survival – preservation of the language, the faith, and the land – were to be the vocation of each individual, each family, and every institution. The Quebec church slammed the door on the revelations of science, but it took hold, to aid its corporatist vision, of a political role it was not to relinquish until the Quiet Revolution beginning in 1960.

Even so, the Canadian New World experience from early on was one which called upon meritocratic values and a uniting of daily life with spiritual meaning. In English Canada, evidence of these qualities appeared early in the literature. T.C. Haliburton in *The Clockmaker* (1836) and Susanna Moodie in *Roughing It in the Bush* (1850), both published before Darwin's *Origin of the Species* (1859) and before Confederation, suggest a uniquely British North American relation to religious custom and belief. Indeed, Haliburton, in a savagely satirical attack on the U.S. representative, [Uncle] Sam Slick, presents capitalism as U.S. religion. The Catholic priest falls into conversation with Slick and asks him *what he is*, meaning, of course, what church he is affiliated with. Slick replies that he is a clockmaker. Since Sam Slick is symbolic of the U.S. in the book, and since he preaches that time is money, declaring loudly that he cares everything for 'ciphering' (using numbers) and nothing for the classics, Haliburton's point is clear. Sam

Slick is a maker of inferior clocks which he sells by shady and 'hard-sell' methods. When asked his religion, Slick replies he is a clockmaker. He is a symbolic American whose religion is the market economy. v

Mrs. Moodie insists upon a God who informs daily action and sees each sparrow's fall. Through all ill, her God is a source of strength and meaning. Providence, for Mrs. Moodie, is so real a factor in her daily search for virtue and justice that she signals from afar one of the reasons why the Social Gospel, arising out of Europe, the U.S.A. and Canada at the same time, has had its most lasting effect in Canada.

If Conservatism based on both Catholic and Protestant traditions assured the country a view of social hierarchy and government as institutions existing by divine ordinance, and if Liberalism assured a reasonably smooth development of pluralisms, then the CCF/NDP and its progenitors assured the country that the criticism of capitalist power would have a vital Christian content and that the spirit of ecumenism would be native to Canada. The founders of the CCF, of the prairie cooperative organizations, and of Social Gospel institutions often worked hand-in-hand when they were not, in fact, the same people.

The Roman Catholic Church, for the most part little involved in the Social Gospel movement from 1885 to the 1920s, has in our day moved into a position of social concern and, indeed, the Catholic intellectual Gregory Baum makes reference to the Social Gospel in Canada when speaking and writing about the trend to increased social commitment among forces in the Catholic Church.[10]

The Social Gospel movement emerged from a society vexed by the social requirements of Christian teaching in the face of industrialization and the claims of science. The Higher Criticism, as it was called – not unrelated to the work of Darwin and Herbert Spencer – forced questions about literal and conventional interpretations of scripture as bases of belief.

Herbert Spencer, a British philosopher/social scientist who was enormously influential in the 1880s and 1890s, argued a version of Adam Smith economics developed through all aspects of life: evolution was universal; present directions in social development were desirable; government would contract its functions and the state would wither; a kind of 'fittest' in an industrial society would fashion civilization.

Conditions in most industrialized cities didn't, however, seem to verify such optimism. The fact that industrialization had transformed large segments of the population into sub-human 'hands' or wage-slaves provided the basis for intense questioning of the system responsible for such naked, visible exploitation. At the same time, the franchise was expanding, and evangelical faiths were becoming involved with the lot of the less literate, labouring population. The labour question, at the heart of what was called the Social Question, became increasingly insistent.

The Social Gospel movement was essentially a Christian social action movement undertaken to force mitigation of the lives of labouring people and to bring harmony to the social fabric, rent by the increasingly obvious conflicts between the interests of capital and those of labour. The first Canadian Social Gospel novel, *Roland Graeme, Knight,* was published by Agnes Maule Machar, a Kingston woman of letters, in 1892. Subtitled "A Novel of Our Times," Machar's novel is set in the (more industrialized) U.S.A. and takes its name from the Knights of Labour, a workers' organization with considerable strength at the time both in Canada and the U.S.A.

The Social Gospellers believed that harmony between labour and capital could be achieved if the labouring classes would learn the full meaning of Christianity and the owners of capital would learn social responsibility. Their teaching gained supporters because their actions could not help but place the owners and managers of enterprise at a disadvantage when the oppressed, often parlous condition, of the working poor was publicized. In 1918 W.L. Mackenzie King's Social Gospel book *Industry and Humanity* could preach the need for harmony and balance between the contending forces and be considered a significant contribution. But in 1920, Salem Bland, an influential Methodist clergyman, could produce a passionately felt and argued book, *The New Christianity*, with quite another theme. Richard Allen writes that Bland's central theme "was that the processes of industrial and social consolidation, the growth of organized labour, and the spread of sociological ideas, especially in the church, spelled the end of the old order of capitalism and Protestantism which had dominated most of western Christendom for three centuries."[11]

Maintaining a strongly Social Gospel line, Bland argued that capitalism stood in the way of a new Christianity of democracy and brotherhood and so had to be extinguished. For many Social Gospellers salvation may have meant a place in the heavenly order, but it most certainly meant the establishment of a just and good relation among people on earth as taught by the example of Jesus Christ. According to Bland, labour Christianity would be born in a new structure of organized worship. Though all Social Gospellers didn't go as far as he did, they all insisted upon the divine relevance of the word of Jesus as its effect was manifested in the world.

Though no one appears to have become jittery about King's *Industry and Humanity*, the appearance of *The New Christianity* made some people nervous. Lieutenant Colonel Hamilton, intelligence and liaison officer with the R.C.M.P., wrote to T. Albert Moore, head of the Methodist Department of Evangelism and Social Service, asking him, in effect, to produce a review of Bland's book that would dampen response to it. T. Albert Moore cooperated.[12] The Social Gospel movement didn't stop as a result of that kind of interference, though a new social order wasn't constructed in place of the old and the Social Gospel was slowly transformed and absorbed into the larger society.

At a time when individualistic rapacity and the pendulum swing in the Canadian dialectic towards non-communitarian values seemed strong, the Protestant churches of Canada, labour representatives, and many others moved to redress the balance. The Communist Party of Canada was founded in 1921, attracting people of conscience who were growing pessimistic about the possibility of the New Christianity and enthusiastic about the Russian Revolution of 1917 and its potential. A.E. Smith, a Social Gospel activist, records his 'conversion' to Communism:

> I began to preach about the great events taking place in Russia and about the great storehouse of truth I had found. I was only a preacher of the truth. I did not make the truth. I was simply telling the truth to the people. I began where I was. I saw that Jesus was a Communist. I linked his life with the old prophets, the great preachers of the Old Testament, who were early Communists. Of course they were not scientific but they stood for the principles of communism. They practised common ownership, and they believed in the Communist maxims: "From each according to his ability, to each according to his need" and "He who will not work, neither shall he eat."[13]

Others who remained Social Gospellers found a place in the CCF. The Communist Party and the CCF differed, disagreed, and fought bitterly. But both insisted upon ideas that called unrestricted free enterprise to account for degradation and poverty among the population. So powerful was the criticism of capitalist free enterprise that legislative forces moved after 1935 to study the nature of Canadian society, to implement systems of security and social encouragement, and to bring about structures that, by 1970, had become characteristic, in many minds, of the Canadian identity.

But churches in Canada had undergone intense scrutiny, significant loss of adherents, and a secularizing and ecumenicizing process that both weakened some conventional aspects of their message and strengthened their credibility as social institutions. It might be fair to say that between 1945 and 1985 the churches were forced through a process of renewal that they could neither have foretold nor prepared for, and that the process left them uncertain and lean.

While the population at large moved away from organized religion, doubts about the place of faith in the twentieth century were broadcast far and wide. After 1945, the world was totally transformed by the presence of potential nuclear holocaust, of high living standards in a world of technology and computer advances, birth control, intense mass communications, increased longevity, and the division of the world into two armed camps – one of which has increasing power over the lives of the Canadian people. An array of forces has seemed to improve the lives of Canadians while increasing the role of individualism here – from increased provincial power and regional conflict, to pornography and violence in art, to increased claims for the central importance of free enterprise. Another product is the expansion of religious groups and rhetoric that equates the Christian message and the corporate message, the word of Jesus and the word of free enterprise capitalism.

The major factor, however, in the transformation of life in the second half of this century has been the division of the world into two camps, and the alliances of the Western nations with the U.S. and its vision of the good life, a vision of society shaped by free enterprise capitalism obsessively exploiting developing nations and increasing wealth at the centres of empire. In recent years, different centres throughout the empire have become competing focusses of capitalist enterprise – New York, London, Tokyo, West Berlin. A struggle for dominance is going on among the more powerful countries involved.

The establishment of the European Common Market, the 'Big Bang' of deregulation in stock exchanges, the formation of the General Agreement on Tariffs and Trade, privatization of publicly owned companies, and a return to 'private sector' rhetoric are all manifestations of market economy intensification – intensification, that is, of the belief that the rule of law, international relations, and concepts of morality and justice must be governed by the driving incentive of the maximization of profits. For Canada the *de facto* primacy of the market economy is everywhere evident, as is the increasing domination of this country's ruling mechanisms by the U.S.A.

As far as the churches and spiritual life are concerned, U.S. domination has had two significant effects. On the one hand, individual liberation has offered examples to both thought and action in Canadian churches. The huge influx of "draft dodgers" during the Viet Nam War was actively supported by churches as an example of the activity of "individual conscience." Most of the draft resistors were not in conflict with the U.S. market economy or with U.S. imperialism in general; rather, they disliked personal involvement with Viet Nam. In one way, the Canadian churches were actively supporting the immigration to Canada of people who epitomized U.S. individualism, and they were doing so as a form of resistance to a particular, obnoxious representation of U.S. policy.

On the other hand, Canadians and Canadian church people have refused to see the U.S. as a Christian power in conflict with godless Communism, the evil empire. The churches have slowly had to bear witness to U.S. support for dictatorships and regimes based on violence and terrorism, as well as watch the active U.S. destabilization and overthrow of freely elected governments. As a result, churches in Canada have found themselves increasingly in alliance with the very governments and people the U.S. is helping to oppress and crush.

At home, led partly by the criticism of U.S. oppression of small countries in Central and South America, the churches have found some of the same analysis applies here. If the U.S. wishes to keep Central and South America open to U.S. capital and U.S. exploitation of both resources and markets, then why should problems Canada faces have essentially different form or character? The attack on unionism in Canada, the slow assault on social insurance structures, the move towards a Free Trade zone for North America, are all less furious manifestations of policy in Central and South America: an attempt to institute a harsh society based on wealth, intense competition, denial of universal human rights and law, and outright oppression of whole segments of the population.

Surprisingly, almost unconsciously, the Canadian churches find themselves awakened and called upon as at the time of the Social Gospel movement – to lead, join alliances, and to reconsider the meaning of their vocation. The Roman Catholic Church in Canada, this time, is active, aware, and often provides leadership against the pendulum swing back to individualism and free enterprise exploitation. Perhaps the presence of Canadian Catholics throughout Central and South America has helped to encourage the Catholic Church in Canada to a new activism as well as a new perception of power in the world.

Religion in Canada has been closely tied to the political life of the country. Though there have been examples of unsavoury collaboration with reactionary governments here, the churches can be argued to have been mainly communitarian. Even when the Church in Quebec worked closely with repressive and reactionary governments there, its policy was anti-materialist, anti-atheist, and anti-Protestant. The reactionary Conservatism of Quebec Catholicism was the opposite of individualist – and it squarely opposed the Liberal reactionary force that claimed to be liberationist and progressive.

Despite, then, their difficulty with some Marxist influence in reform movements, the advent of 'liberation theology,' and Establishment resistance to strong labour organizations, the peace-loving religious groups in Canada have found their allegiances more and more drawn to "the preferential option for the poor." That attraction is perfectly plausible and credible in terms of the Canadian dialectic. But we have yet to see what the outcome will be if big capital and the Canadian churches meet in head-on conflict for the first time in our history.

CHAPTER SIX

Religion, Economics, and Social Structure

*R*eligious, political, and economic forces in contest have formed a unique pattern in Canada and have expressed themselves enduringly in our community life and political process without being precisely characterized by Canadian (or other) commentators. Probably the best way to get at the full implications of the opposition is to examine the resilient set of arguments Max Weber set out in 1904-05 about the close connection between Protestantism and capitalism in his famous work entitled *The Protestant Ethic and the Spirit of Capitalism.*

Weber suggested that Roman Catholicism has been less sympathetic than Protestantism to capitalist values. Protestants and Catholics both like and dislike the argument; sociologists and historians praise and condemn it. But no one denies the compelling nature of Weber's ideas. His thesis was a significant attempt to explain how the Western world moved into the forms of production that supported the development of a technological society while the rest of the world lagged behind, even when it had developed many of the scientific ideas and concepts necessary.

The spirit of capitalism, Weber insisted, is unique to the West, and represented a significant break from traditional types of economic activity. All ages have had greed, have had trade, production and accumulation of wealth. But, according to Weber, something unique happened in Western Europe from the 1500s on with the Protestant Reformation. What he describes compels our attention because we can see evidence of it all around us today.

The spirit of capitalism depends upon an organized labour force and the continuous investment of capital, neither of which existed in the 'traditional economy.' But most characteristically and definitively, it depends upon the continuous reproduction of wealth, the continual investment and reinvestment of capital in order simply to accumulate, so that acquisition itself, not acquisition in order to be able to use and enjoy the good things of the world, becomes its own end. In Canadian terms, the concept relates directly to our major dialectic. Do we as a people simply release energy to perfect the spirit of capitalism and unimpeded individualistic accumulation and increase of wealth for its own sake, or do we use wealth in order to create a community rich in social well-being, secure in reasonable enjoyment of the good things of the world?

Weber theorized that characteristics of Protestantism, growing out of the Reformation, formed the ground out of which the spirit of capitalism grew dominant. This isn't the place to argue the universal truth of Weber's analysis. The characteristics of Protestantism that he says became the seedbed for the spirit of capitalism do, however, help us to understand the dialectic in Canada as it relates to Protestantism and Catholicism here. During the Reformation, the Protestant faiths broke away from Roman Catholicism, relinquishing traditional formulations of a relation with God through the intermediary of Church and priest and emphasizing the individual's perception. At the same time, Protestantism released the individual into wordly activity as a positive good.

Luther, according to Weber, created something new: "the valuation of the fulfillment of duty in worldly affairs as the highest form which moral activity of the individual could assume."[1] Luther's idea of the "calling" made worldly activity so significant spiritually it freed believers to the point that their demonstrations of wealth and worldly success could be offered as signs the people involved were in a state of grace.

As Weber had it, the Protestant reformers, especially Calvin, lifted asceticism from the religious sphere and set it free in the secular sphere. Energy formerly employed to seek out God's Will and learn discipline in His service could be released in the service of the accumulation of wealth. Before long, according to Weber, wealth and success began to be pursued for their own sakes, with ascetic fervour – an activity we are familiar with in contemporary life. The argument mirrors a principal view that has been dominant in Canada – that the English Protestant part of the country is dynamic, hard-working, and economically successful, while the Francophone Catholic part is inefficient, slothful, and economically backward. English Canadian literature, for instance, commonly contrasts the dark, romantic, emotional, inefficient Francophone with the blond, realistic, rational, efficient English Canadian.

The individualistic nature of faith and salvation created in Protestant belief, Weber believed, forced adherents of Calvinism, Pietism, Methodism, the Baptist sects and their related faiths to seek intensely for ways to reveal in the world that the individual had been saved. Having abandoned the Roman Catholic cycle of sin, confession, contrition, penance, and absolution-from-sin, the Protestant sects had no institutionalized *machinery* to provide them with publicly credible means of asserting absolution from sin and achievement of a state of grace. They therefore sought a systematic, methodical way of living to be sure of salvation, to be sure they were in a state of grace, to be born again, to be – like Christ himself – individually infused by God with his approval, and even, His Selfhood.

Catholicism offered the believer a traditionally inter-preted faith, communitarian existence in the spirit (as well as individual salvation), a Conservative hierarchy with levels of responsibility, and an on-going machinery of purification. Protestantism's individualization of the relation to God, the compulsion to be able – individually – to manifest salvation, and the belief that worldly calling related intimately to spiritual legitimacy, prepared the way for Protestantism to be the vehicle in which capitalism manoeuvred into modern life, according to Weber.

But Weber went a step farther. The very nature of the relation between Protestantism and capitalism he believed, required that capitalism destroy Christian belief in order to create an environment in which the uninhibited making of money could become a mass phenomenon pursued with religious zeal as an entirely virtuous end in itself.

Weber quotes an ambiguous statement by John Wesley, the founder of Methodism, on how the success of capitalism seemed to guarantee the destruction of faith:

> I fear, wherever riches have increased, the essence of religion has decreased in the same proportion. Therefore, I do not see how it is possible, in the nature of things, for any revival of true religion to continue long. For religion must necessarily produce both industry and frugality, and these cannot but produce riches. But as riches increase, so will pride, anger, and love of the world in all its branches. How then is it possible that Methodism, that is, a religion of the heart, though it flourishes now as a green bay tree, should continue in

this state? For the Methodists in every place grow diligent and frugal; consequently they increase in goods. Hence they proportionately increase in pride, in anger, in the desire of the flesh, the desire of the eyes, and the pride of life. So, although the form of religion remains, the spirit is swiftly vanishing away. Is there no way to prevent this – this continual decay of pure religion? We ought not to prevent people from being diligent and frugal: *we must exhort all Christians to gain all they can, and to save all they can; that is, in effect, to grow rich.*[2]

Wesley may have had a divided mind; Weber did not. He wrote:

... when asceticism was carried out of monastic cells into everyday life, and began to dominate worldly morality, it did its part in building the tremendous cosmos of the modern economic order. This order is now bound to the technical and economic conditions of machine production.... Today the spirit of religious asceticism – whither who knows? – has escaped from the cage. But victorious capitalism, since it rests on mechanical foundations, needs its support no longer.... Where the fulfillment of the calling cannot directly be related to the highest spiritual and cultural values, or when, on the other hand, it need not be felt simply as economic compulsion, the individual generally abandons the attempt to justify it at all. In the field of its highest development, in the United States, the pursuit of wealth, stripped of its religious and ethical meaning, tends to become associated with purely mundane passions .... [3]

In Canada, unlike in the U.S., the situation was characterized by tensions more than by unanimity. The conditions caused by the Conquest of New France, English-speaking

Protestant dominance, and the rejection of the French Revolution by the Church in Quebec produced a world which in many ways mirrors Max Weber's theory, and so that theory is peculiarly relevant to an examination of Canadian identity and the dialectic characteristic of that identity. George Grant argues, in addition, the *kind* of Protestantism that came to Canada from England was caught in the net of traditions that slowed the process of secularization Weber describes. For Grant, then, (and for commentators like Gad Horowitz) Canada had a basis upon which to erect a community and an identity quite separate from those of the United States.

Whatever the basis of their theorizing, however, no Canadian commentators deny a long visible historic fact: enterpreneurship, risk-taking, scientific initiative, and industrial development were demonstrably in the hands of the Protestant English Canadians in league with U.S. interests. Francophone Catholics remained, for the most part, devout, communitarian, even corporatist, simple, and un-modern.

Even today, unemployment in Quebec is usually double that in Protestant Ontario, though the myth of the inefficient Quebecois is dying. Until the Quiet Revolution in 1960, and even after it, Quebec rejected Protestant individualism and seemed to find capitalist accumulation alien to its character. The reason may lie with the nationalist analysis of Michel Brunet or the Marxist analysis of Stanley Ryerson, but there can be no question that religion – the Protestantism of Anglophone Canada and the Catholicism of Francophone Quebec – existed in relation to specific economic forms described by Weber.

The social structures that resulted produced a stereotypical colonial capitalist structure in English Canada and what seemed much closer to a "traditional economy" in Quebec. Whatever other forces were at work, the dialectic in Canada had a level of tension that set the Anglophone against the Francophone culture. In 1937, Felix Antoine Savard could write the great novel *Menaud, Maître Draveur* in which Anglophone strangers were entering Quebec, dislocating the people, and alienating their land, while the farmers were too unknowing to respond to the challenge. In 1945, Hugh MacLennan's *Two Solitudes* presented the stereotypical Protestant capitalist at work, while the "traditional" Quebec priest attempted to shelter his flock from the destructive values being introduced by the modern world. Also in 1945 Gabrielle Roy's *The Tin Flute* portrayed a desperate Quebec family quite untouched by any comprehension of the spirit of capitalism; a single character, Jean Levesque, symbolically dresses in English-style clothes, manifests extremely destructive secular individualism, and is driven by an obsession to achieve financial success.

The major conflict in Frederick Philip Grove's *Fruits of the Earth* (1933) and *Master of the Mill* (1944) develops because the protagonists, representatives of Anglophone Canadian power, having completely adopted secularized individualism, cannot balance the demands of the spirit of capitalism and the requirement for humane community. Their desires for dynastic continuity and for community values based on traditional ideas of responsibility are smashed against, first, the image of the wheel, and then the image of capitalist technological dominance – the vertically integrated transnational corporation.

The two cultures have shifted significantly since the beginning of the Quiet Revolution in 1960. If the death of the old Conservatism has reorganized the dialectic in Canada-U.S. terms, the dialectic between English and French Canada has shifted dramatically, too. Quebec has been able, in an astonishingly short time, to divest itself of clerical control, and even clerical participation, in the culture. Shortly before the Quiet Revolution in the days of Duplessis, a powerful Church managed an apparently docile and devout population; the values of the faith, the language, and the land were preached, and the Catholic ideals of Lionel Groulx, the great nationalist priest, appeared to hold sway. But Quebec was not living with its back to the world: large corporate interests (often U.S.-based) were exploiting Quebec raw materials. Enterprise was profitable for its mostly Anglophone owners, positions of supervision also being mostly in the hands of Anglophones.

The economic picture revealed by the Royal Commission on Bilingualism and Biculturalism (1965) showed an economically oppressed Francophone population, but an Anglophone population living within Quebec as a more or less isolated modern economic community. Economic managers might have been subsidiary to Toronto or Chicago, but were little more hampered in Quebec than if they had been located in Winnipeg or Sudbury. The commission revealed that the highest earning group in Quebec was unilingual Anglophone. The next highest earning group was also Anglophone, bilingual Anglophone. Third came bilingual Francophones; fourth unilingual Francophones; and lowest in earning power was a group made up of recent immigrants and native peoples. People in the rest of Canada were surprised at the revelation. Most of them were unilingual in English-speaking provinces, and the idea of being almost at the bottom of the earning groups in their provinces because of the language they spoke made them see for the first time the complaint of Quebec Francophones.

After the Quiet Revolution, different forces in Quebec rallied to define new political directions. Attempts were made by theorists and political groups to create significant socialist movements. The attempts failed. In the political formulations leading to the launching of the Parti Quebecois, Left elements (as at the foundation of the CCF 40 years before) attempted to include serious criticisms of free enterprise capitalism. But they did not succeed, even to the extent those forces succeeded with the Regina Manifesto of the CCF in 1933. The revolution was to be one that finished off clerical domination of Quebec life once and for all, that reorganized the economic status of those in Quebec whose first language was French, and that asserted the legitimacy of Quebec so that aspirations to political independence seemed quite reasonable both within the province and by other provinces.

Though Hydro Quebec has been formed, medical and age insurance have been implemented, and the French language has been given respect it did not possess, the revolution that has been achieved in Quebec has been the move of the whole population into the Liberal Capitalist (free enterprise) orbit of the larger capitalist system. Having removed the traditional brakes upon continentalist integration, Quebec is ready to present its population to the world as North American like the others. (If René Levesque could reply to that statement, he might explode: "So you think the Quebecois should go on hiding in the skirts of parish priests in starving farming communities so you can say Canada isn't racing after the buck the way the U.S. does?" Unfortunately, we cannot hear, now, from René Levesque.)

The facts can be looked at in terms of the fundamental Canadian dialectic. After the defeat of the Parti Quebecois a Liberal Party took power in Quebec, but it is now an economically Conservative government that does not find repugnant the governments of Ronald Reagan, Margaret Thatcher or Brian Mulroney. The premier of the province, Robert Bourassa, is married into one of the wealthy Quebec capitalist families, and leads a government actively enthusiastic to have a Free Trade agreement with the U.S.A.

All other things being equal, Quebec's affinity for the U.S. and Levesque's wish for a free trade area (enthusiastically adopted by his successor) would be simply an interesting aspect of the Quebec personality. But since the Quiet Revolution, Quebec has become a Liberal society, in arts and literature, in political direction, in the separation of religion and the state, and in social behaviour. In terms of the Canadian dialectic, Quebec is now an individualist, free-enterprise society [¹] in which the values set out by Max Weber as characteristic of capitalist society fit without chafing. In Quebec, the American side of the dialectic has taken full power, as it has among so-called Conservatives in English Canada. If, in order to strike a balance, it is necessary for the churches in the rest of Canada to see themselves in conflict with the federal government, such a role will not be so easy in Quebec. For, in that province, the Church has been ousted from close participation in social, political, and economic life. The population of Quebec might not regard with favour a spiritual organization wanting, so soon, to try for influence in the secular sphere.

The labour unions can and will have some effect in resisting the alienation and atomization of the society. But they are not strong enough to provide a balance in and of themselves. The NDP, moreover, is not firmly enough rooted in Quebec soil nor convinced enough there that the New Liberalism and its free trade banner should be resisted. Ironically, Quebec, which for so many years resisted liberalization, is now a leader in the classic Liberal process of the Adam Smith kind, a process that will open Canadian borders, flatten cultural differences, and result in what Weber called Protestant capitalism in "its highest development," engaging in "the pursuit of wealth; stripped of its religious and ethical meaning . . . associated with purely mundane passions . . . ."

Around 1935, Lionel Groulx observed that English Canada was slowly losing ties with Great Britain and could only, inevitably, slip into the United States. He warned the people of Quebec to plan for that day and to prepare to go it alone in North America. Groulx's comments were astute. The tie with Great Britain, we are now beginning to see, was not simply a tie of colonial sentiment. In relation to the Canadian dialectic, it stood for an ideological position of independence, however mythical and impossible to maintain, because it permitted Canadians to claim a distinct otherness from the U.S.A. Groulx said that if English Canada could not develop a claim to distinctness without the prop of Great Britain, removal of the prop would result in the end of English Canada.

Audacious Quebec nationalist historian, devout Catholic, determined Francophone that he was, Groulx, however, could not have imagined that events in the country might have shifted so much that Quebec might well be in the same condition as English Canada, in serious danger of economic annexation by the U.S. When he wrote, the clerical hand was firm in Quebec and the province's solidarity seemed unshakeable. Very shortly after his death in 1967, a Quebec appeared that he would not have recognized. Doubtless Max Weber would have seen clearly the transformations potential in "traditional" Quebec society within the larger context of Liberal Capitalist Democracy and its secular free enterprise philosophy.

Quebec society has leaped a phase in Weber's analysis. He traced the move from Catholicism to intense ascetic Protestantism directed towards worldly success and then into religion-destroying capitalism. In Quebec the population has turned away from Catholicism, embracing secular capitalism in one move. The result is that Quebec is, in some ways, the most Liberal of Liberal communities in Canada: the new Conservatism is called, correctly, in Quebec, the new Liberalism.

Seen in terms of the shift of Canadian political Conservatism into crude free enterprise capitalism, the shift to Liberalism in Quebec is threatening for the survival of the country. Both factors have, historically, provided weight to the communitarian, non-Liberal capitalist, independentist side of the Canadian dialectic. Both are, at least for the present, absorbed into the other side of the dialectic. Whether Canada can survive the two defections is a serious question.

CHAPTER SEVEN

Quebec and Canadian Identity

The existence of a Catholic Francophone population and a Protestant Anglophone one has significantly shaped Canadian identity. George Grant tended to argue, rather exclusively, that a Conservative, communitarian force in English society formed a culture significantly different and more humane than U.S. culture and that the decline of that force has doomed Canada. Stanley Ryerson and other Marxists argued that the values Grant cherishes had to be destroyed by developing European and U.S. capitalism, that Quebec – a significant part of the dialectic – was pressed into an unequal union because of British capitalist power, and that Canadian identity is an idealized version of reality increasingly difficult to maintain in the face of the continuing development of capitalism. But since Quebec early responded to the necessity of living with a predominant Anglophone fact in league with British and U.S. imperialism, the existence of Quebec has, if anything, heightened its importance to the dialectic.

Since 1960 in Quebec all forms of individual expression, of what might be called "self-expression," have expanded since the removal of religious corporatist pressure, but without so far erasing the achievements of consciousness and identity forged over two centuries. Quebec can be seen as a community which, from the Conquest on, moved into forms and concepts of religious corporatism, for unity and defence, until the time of the Quiet Revolution. Corporatism in Quebec is often seen in English Canada as having been a repressive, backward, stultifying force, as in many ways it no doubt was. But it also served a purpose in that it permitted the survival of French Canada. Corporatism, therefore, must be carefully examined in the Canadian context. Many Canadians think, correctly, of corporatism in its relation to Nazi Germany and Fascist Italy, but do not understand its existence in the Quebec context.

Quite simply, corporatism is a view of society which sees the whole community as a single body, all parts of which contribute to and are part of the health and function of the whole. The whole may, as in Nazism, be directed to the elevation of a supreme race, rendering all others subservient or non-existent. The whole may, as in Fascism, be directed to an attempt to organize corporations for economic activity so that the whole population works with concerted direction. Corporatism may also, in a religious society, try to direct the lives and activities of the population to a good described ultimately in terms of a theory of transcendent truth. That kind of corporatism is probably present to some degree in any theocratic or strongly theologically motivated society.

In Quebec, the struggle of the Church for political and social power may be analysed in any number of ways, but its result was corporatist. One of the first dispensations the English conqueror gave the Quebecois was the right to practise their own religion. In a growing ocean of Protestantism, Catholicism in Quebec became related to the survival of the race, the preservation of the language, and the guardianship of the land. Though nothing as structured or visible as Italian Fascism's 22 corporations (1934) was ever created in Quebec, yet the power of the Church in government, education, and social services created, in effect, a corporatist purpose for Quebec. On the one hand, that purpose may be summed up in the inward-looking phrase "la survivance." On the other hand, it also embraced the outward-looking impulse of a missionary vocation. As Mgr. L.-F.-R. Laflèche wrote in 1866, Quebec had a mission entrusted to it by Providence:

> Every individual in a family, every family in a nation, every nation in mankind – each has a special predestination . . . . The mission with which Providence entrusted French Canadians is basically religious in nature: it is, namely, to convert the unfortunate infidel local population to Catholicism, and to expand the Kingdom of God by developing a predominantly Catholic nationality.[1]

The sense of special vocation and special character affected Quebec's relation with the rest of Canada, and not only in matters of religion, for corporatism can wear many masks: economic, political, religious, military, and cultural. By its very nature, it mingles with all aspects as it gains power. Historians trace the increasing influence of the Catholic Church in Quebec to the severe buffetings the province suffered at the hands of English-language and Protestant interests. A dialectic continued for more than two hundred years in Quebec's relation with English Canada, and the face Quebec often showed the rest of Canada was a corporatist face, moving the province towards a single goal sanctified by Providence.

While that idea seems strange to English Canadians with a Liberal and pluralist sense of society, the general idea of corporatism should not be completely unfamiliar, even though in times of Liberal philosophy corporatism is considered evil because it offers, superficially observed, a totally different set of values than is accepted by the mainstream.

The general idea should be familiar to Canadians because the laments, theories, and postulates of many of the first-order thinkers in Canada have been based on their conviction that a *new corporatism* has gained power in the world: free enterprise capitalism, driven by the ineluctable force of technology in the hands of Liberal ideologists. All social forces are increasingly devoted to a single corporate reality, the efficient and unhindered operation of free enterprise capitalism directing the means of production towards the accumulation of private wealth and power. Under the new corporatism, the state exists to facilitate the operation of free enterprise capitalism; the churches exist to adorn and sanctify it; the culture exists to manifest its ubiquity and single-mindedness. For two centuries the existence of a theologically oriented Quebec culture stood in the way of the new corporatism. After 1960, that condition changed.

The Conquest of 1760 and the Treaty of Paris in 1763 did not force the new subjects of the British Crown into a mold desired by the conquerer because U.S. expansionist aspirations were growing evident and the U.S. war of independence was on the horizon. A brief 13 years spanned the time between the Treaty of Paris and the U.S. Declaration of Independence. As a result, the treatment of the conquered in Quebec by the Quebec Act of 1774 granted dispensations to the Quebecois in order to woo their loyalty to Britain and provide them with a basis to reject the blandishments of the U.S.A.

Succeeding legislation and day-to-day treatment of the Quebec people provided for a general atmosphere of peace and tranquility. Though historians argue about the feelings of the Quebecois, the U.S. invaders were not joined in significant numbers by the people of Quebec in 1775, nor did the Quebecois support U.S. invaders in any significant way in the War of 1812. The Rebellions of 1837, however, which occurred in both Upper and Lower Canada, introduced a shift.

Lord Durham's Report on the Rebellions led to the union of Upper and Lower Canada with the stated purpose of assimilating the Francophone population into Anglophone Canada. The tenacity of the Quebecois in relation to their own culture was unflinching. They seemed, in fact, to respond with cultural activity designed to ensure survival. One of the monuments of that effort was Quebec's (and Canada's) first major history, the three-volume *Histoire du Canada* by Francois Xavier Garneau.

A Liberal, Garneau was no parochial colonial by the time he came to his work of history in the 1840s. Educated to be a lawyer, he had read widely in the great works of French and English thought. He had travelled to England where he observed the British parliament at work, and to France where he observed the National Assembly in its legislative activity. He discussed with Poles he met in England the problems of peoples subordinated in constitutional systems designed by others. He developed a history he believed recognized the identity, the value, and the tenacity of the Quebecois as a people with a distinct personality. Turning upside down the idea that national personality is forged in great struggles leading to victory and predominance, Garneau told his people that great nobility can be expressed in defeat and despite subordination:

When we contemplate the history of Canada as a whole, from the time of Champlain till our own day, we first remark its two great divisions – the period of French supremacy, and that of British domination. The annals of the former are replete with the incidents of wars against the savages and the people of the conterminous British colonies, since become the United States; the other portion is signalised by parliamentary antagonism of the colonists to all infractions of their nationality and designs against their religion. The difference of the arms used defensively during those two periods, shows the Canadian nation under two very distinct aspects; but it is the second epoch which, naturally enough, may most interest the existing generation. There is something at once noble and touching in the spectacle of a people defending the nationality of their ancestors; that sacred heritage which no race, how degraded soever, has ever yet repudiated. Never did cause of loftier character or more holy nature inspire a heart rightly placed, or better merit the sympathies of all generous minds.[2]

Claiming for the Quebecois an ancestral, Gallic power, Garneau saw them as capable of prevailing against all odds:

The nationality of the great people from whom they are descended, animating them under menaces, causes the rejection of all capitulations offered to them; their Gallic nature, while separating them from phlegmatic races, sustains them in circumstances hopeless for others. In fine, that cohesive force, peculiar to their moral temperament, develops itself in proportion to the efforts made to overcome it.[3]

The general resistance to assimilation in Quebec strengthened clerical forces and helped develop politicians of stature, so that by the time of Confederation, Quebec had affirmed its Catholic and Francophone identity in a way that could not be denied. Its leaders were able to assert Quebec reality in the move toward a national, post-colonial vision.

Canadians tend to forget the significance of the fact that the union of the Canadas (essentially, the union of Ontario and Quebec intended to assimilate the Quebecois into English Canada) remained in effect until 1867. The Quebecois were generally jubilant about Confederation: after 27 years without a government of their own, they entered a new formation

that not only gave them a provincial government with juris-
diction over important elements of life, but also gave them
guarantees of language, faith, and educational freedom na-
tionally. Despite very important gains, their jubilation was
not to last long. Scarcely a quarter of a century passed before
the Quebecois began to see disturbing signs of Anglophone
domination. The hanging of Louis Riel and then the long
conflict over the right of Francophones in Manitoba to be
educated in French spoke plainly to them. (Ironically, the law
that denied education in French in Manitoba was not declared
invalid until the 1970s.) ✓

Forces in Quebec had, therefore, to fear Western expansion and settlement and to doubt the terms of Confederation
were being carried out. In the same quarter century, the call
to Empire in support of English adventure resulting in the
Boer War further troubled the people in Quebec. In fairly
rapid succession after Confederation and into the twentieth
century they faced the hanging of Riel, the Manitoba Schools
Question, the Boer War, the Ontario Schools Question, and
First World War conscription, all issues that invited them to
believe the Confederation agreements and documents would
not be honoured in letter or in spirit as far as French Canada
was concerned.

As if to confirm the postulates of Francois Xavier
Garneau quoted earlier, the Quebecois, from 1890 on, cut off
from serious national political power, built upon the sense of
missionary vocation so that Mgr. Laflèche's comments already
quoted were not tributary to Quebec thought but mainstream.
Indeed, out of that concept of a Providential mission, a confes-
sional literature was born in the early twentieth century and
enjoyed wide distribution; Church and social organizations
of extensive influence increased power. Their histories have
not been adequately treated. English Canadians, partly as a
result, are almost always taken aback when they hear or read
statements about Quebec mission. Mgr. Pâquet's statement

of 1909 crystallizes the ideas and attitudes of the growth and development of missionary vocation that did not begin seriously to wane until after the Second World War:

> We have the privilege of being entrusted with the social priesthood granted only to select peoples. I cannot doubt that this religious and civilizing mission is the true vocation and the special vocation of the French race in America. Yes, let us not forget, we are not only a civilized race, we are pioneers of a civilization; we are not only a religious people, we are messengers of the spirit of religion; we are not only the dutiful sons of the Church, we are, or we should be, numbered among its zealots, its defenders, and its apostles. Our mission is less to handle capital than to stimulate ideas; less to light the furnaces of factories than to maintain and spread the glowing fires of religion and thought, and to help them cast their light into the distance.[4]

Philosophy in Quebec has had a close relation with religion. In New France, philosophy mirrored the arguments of the old continent until the French Revolution, when many of the French clergy made their way to Canada and began work that helped to shape philosophical thought in Quebec in the nineteenth century. After the French Revolution, Quebec not only faced the new, expansionist U.S.A. but a restructured France in which Church and State were rigidly separated. Quebec revealed a conservative philosophical face for the first half of the nineteenth century and only moved as global pressure forced change. Generally, when it came, adaptation to philosophical ideas in Canada related as much to the global assault on Catholicism as it did to peculiar needs in the new country.

In 1879, the papal encyclical of Pope Leo XIII, *Aeternis Patris*, recommended the philosophy of Saint Thomas Aquinas as a source of knowledge for Roman Catholics. A Thomist revival which had begun before the middle of the century was given official sanction by the encyclical. Aquinas was adaptable to contemporary problems because he had suggested a useful distinction between the modern realm of reason and the traditional realm of faith. In nature, according to Aquinas, reason and philosophy held sway; but in *supernature* faith and philosophy held sway. Leslie Armour and Elizabeth Trott have cited three major reasons for the Thomist revival: first, the rise of history as an ultimately scientific discipline threatened faith which relied on transcendent assurances of the meaning of history. Secondly, evolutionary theory suggested the mutability of all things, including religious belief. Thirdly, mechanistic physics separated religion from a belief system fast becoming based upon methods of reason alone.[5]

Thomist philosophy was complex, but basically it offered the argument that *essence* differed from *existence* and that the human soul was a subsistent form which united with matter to constitute human nature. Clearly the argument was brilliant, at the same time as it skated on thin ice, for such a postulate was good only as long as the reasoner was willing and able to grant the ultimate role and final supremacy of faith. As Armour and Trott have said:

> The separation of faith and reason was made by insisting that (1) faith and reason cannot contradict each other, (2) not all elements of the faith can be demonstrated, and (3) when there is an apparent conflict which cannot be resolved by categorizing the element of faith as belonging to the sphere of the undemonstratable, one should assume that there has been a mistake of reasoning and begin over again, with a different sort of reasoning.[6]

When faith is no longer possible, the separation of the realms of reason and faith become the basis for excluding the realm of faith as anything but worn-out hocus pocus. With the Reformation, Protestantism separated from the Catholic cycle of sin and purification, elevated "calling" in the world to theological place, transferred asceticism from the religious to the secular sphere, and developed proofs of grace from success in the world. After that, as Weber claimed, capitalism dispenses, in any significant way, with any religious need whatever. Thomist ideas served to prepare Catholic Quebec for similar development. When faith was removed as the final arbiter of meaning, reason was left exposed to the full power of secularized Protestant thought.

Catholicism and philosophy in Quebec developed from Aquinas and attempted to balance and integrate the spheres of faith and reason. For many years the attempt bore fruit. Nothing, perhaps, could have warned the Quebecois of the stresses that would culminate in the Quiet Revolution, stresses that both mirrored and manifested larger forces at work in the world.

After the First World War, clerical influence continued to dominate in Quebec for good and ill. With the Second World War, conscription again caused bitter division between Quebec and English Canada. Post-war television provided pictures of affluent North America against which the Quebecois could compare their own community. Post-war decolonization movements around the world introduced the concept of "negritude" and saw the Quebecois develop the concept of white niggers of America. In all cases, as they related to their province, the Quebecois could see a combination of unjust dominance by the English and the Church's refusal to work for the amelioration of the earthly lot of the Quebec people. When the change came, it came as a radical secularization and a radical antipathy to English Canadians.

In meeting the challenge of a Protestant, materialistic, technological, and worldly ideology outside Quebec, the people of the province at first retreated, led by clerics whose vision of eternity and God could challenge Liberal materialism. But when the Quebecois turned upon their religious leaders and upon the symbols of their materialist oppression, they were left with only two fundamental choices: independence and closely guarded self-sufficiency or economic partnership with the U.S. and significantly loosened ties with English Canada. An architect of the Meech Lake Accord and an enthusiastic supporter of Free Trade with the U.S.A., the province is now poised for the assimilation it spent 225 years resisting.

Perhaps that turn of events should not be surprising. The condition of tension in which Quebec lived created what Hubert Aquin, a major twentieth century Quebec writer, called "cultural fatigue" – a condition that sapped the energy and self-assurance of the Quebecois, leaving them fragmented and torn in identity. Facing viciousness about Quebec expressed in Pierre Trudeau's 1962 article called "La nouvelle trahison des clercs," Aquin despaired for Quebec:

> Culturally fatigued and weary, French Canada for a long time has been going through an endless winter; every time the sun breaks through the ceiling of cloud that has obliterated the heavens, in spite of our weakness, our sickness and disillusionment, we start hoping for spring again. French-Canadian culture has long been dying; it makes frequent recoveries, followed by new relapses, and thus leads a precarious existence of fits, starts, and collapses.[7]

Assimilationist pressure always accepts everything about the different community but its difference, as English Canadians well know when they think about the idea in relation to the U.S. U.S. criticisms of Canada, looked at clearly, are criticisms of Canada's failure to be the U.S. In all ways that Canadians and Canada satisfy U.S. ideas of its own interests and act in the way people from the U.S. would act, Canadians are considered, to use the American phrase, "just like us."

Aquin himself mirrored the peculiar tensions in Quebec culture. He could not accept the old Roman Catholicism, and he hoped for a revitalized, independent Quebec within a capitalist system which could not, by the very nature of its operation, permit independence of the kind Aquin envisioned. He was, therefore, a "double agent," as he described the narrator in his novel *Prochain Épisode:* in a way he didn't realize, he was pushing for a style of Quebec's independence which could only take it deeper into assimilationist, integrationist North American. For present dominant power in English Canada wishes to make a compromise with French Canada. French will be accepted increasingly as a national language on the terms that the Quebecois accept Liberal capitalist technology as the religion of the country.

Aquin perceived the dialectic of Quebec's identity within Canada with sharp clarity, and he described, unconsciously, a condition that by the time Quebec had readied itself for assimilation would apply equally as well to the dialectic of Canadian identity within a continental context:

> French Canada, a dying, tired culture, is at square one in politics. Those who have been most successful politically are 'a-nationalists'. They are the ones who have best 'represented' this unrealized, parcelled, and dispossessed people. Success for our federal politicians has depended on their cultural 'dis-integration'. Their 'inexistence' has reflected the constrained culture they represent and which they have almost all been eager to 'fatigue' even more by turning it into folklore so successfully that the federal government, by its very existence, proclaims that there is no longer any dialectical tension between the French- and English-Canadian cultures. The federal government is not the focus of a basic, elemental

struggle; in fact it has never been so, or very rarely. The federal superstructure, in sanctifying the appeasement of French Canada, does not stem from the historical dialectic of the two Canadas, but from a desire to suppress this dialectic, so that Ottawa, a capital between two provinces, rules over ten of them. The political portrait of Ottawa masks the real confrontation in a disguised monolithic regime which legalistically considers French Canada to be one province in ten. The dialectical struggle between the two Canadas does not take place in Ottawa; it is 'depoliticized', at least in the sense that there are no 'institutions' either resulting from it or containing it. The dialectical struggle is in fact taking place elsewhere, almost everywhere, and deep within our consciousness as well. It is not for us to say how it will end, but it is important to know that it is going on and becoming more and more unavoidable. Fatigue, however great, is still not death.[8]

Aquin changed the conclusion he drew above when he committed suicide 15 years after writing the paragraph, in 1977. The election of the Parti Quebecois made him realize that Quebec was deepening, not solving, its problem culturally.

The resonances for Canadian/U.S. relations abound. The 'a-nationalism' of federal politicians is the norm, not the exception. Their constraint of Canadian culture is written large in the battles to develop Canadian cinema, book publishing, broadcasting, educational sources – all of which have been sacrificed to U.S. interests. The federal government, by the stance it takes, proclaims there is no longer any dialectical tension between the Canadian and U.S. cultures. Signs of dialectic, like the Foreign Investment Review Agency and the return to Canadian control of the economy hesitatingly begun by the creation of Petro Canada are ruthlessly erased. By shifting a few words in a major part of Aquin's statement, his assertion can be applied to Canadian/U.S. relations: "The federal superstructure, in sanctifying the political appeasement of the United States, does not stem from the historic dialectic of the two countries, but from a desire to suppress this dialectic, so that Washington, a capital between two countries, rules over them both."

The history of English Canadians has been different from that of French Canadians but it has also shared certain similarities. English Canada's difference from Francophone Canada can be described in the positions of conqueror and conquered. Its similarity can be described in its state of cultural fatigue and the unrelieved pressure upon it of integrationist and assimilationist ideas.

The move by the Quebecois to assume a new position in North America is understandable. Throughout history since the Conquest the Quebecois were not invited into the life and activity of the other provinces, except where small, ineradicable pockets of Francophone populations created leaders and pressure groups. At the time of the launching of the Quiet Revolution, Francophones in Canada, though theoretically full partners in Confederation, were securely locked in their fortress home – the Province of Quebec.

From earliest times, then, Canada presented a unique community. Immigrants from the United Kingdom and the U.S. after 1776 had to be aware of the division North America had experienced. Those who chose to remain in British North America did so because they found the Canadian environment acceptable; others went back to Europe or moved to the U.S.A. Those who remained, as George Grant, Harold Innis and others have claimed, shaped a society that had qualities distinct enough to describe an identity really unique, a Canadian identity. History has given evidence of the continuing dialectic: the struggle of cooperative community against naked capitalist individualism; the struggle of parliamentary constitutionalism against egalitarian, individualistic Republicanism; the struggle of Francophone Catholicism against Anglophone Protestantism; the struggle of a Canadian against a U.S. sense of being; the struggle of centralized federalism against federalized regionalism.

The fortress Quebec built was socially and economically full of contradictions within the dialectic. The Thomist revival in Catholicism carried elements of its own destruction. The communitarian nature of a theological community found itself in contradiction as it fought against community-oriented federal social insurance measures which seemed to threaten Quebec's provincial powers. The rhetoric of Providential mission and a life of simplicity was contradicted by Church-supported state power that abetted large foreign ownership and was content with an exploited population operating at the lowest levels of the economy.

Since 1960 – two hundred years after the Conquest – it has, however, joined the secular free market society. It has, as advocates of its new condition might say, taken its place in twenty-first century society. The new situation could produce the first step on the way to a monolithic North America, a truly 'new corporatism' hateful to behold and worse to live in, as the fundamental dialectic that has given Canada its basis of identity is dissolved in a tidal wave of U.S. power, U.S. culture, U.S. social forms and attitudes to technology, and U.S.-managed individualistic, capitalist free-market economics. Should, on the other hand, a swing of the dialectical pendulum, a shift of national direction come about, Quebec and English Canada could produce something very different. Poised to work together in unity as never before, calling upon resources of shared experience, custom, and values, this country's population could produce a Canada that is vital, unique, and independent as it has not been independent before in its history.

Conclusion

In Canada there has been a movement among the relatively unpropertied for an increasing share of the wealth controlled by the propertied. Because of democratic representation in parliaments and a need on the part of the wealthy to legitimate the Liberal Capitalist system, real advances have been made for ordinary people, without significantly affecting the accumulation of wealth by the propertied. Communitarianism has been strong enough to demand modification of single-minded individualism.

But communitarianism in Canada has never been strong enough to shape Canada's strategies in relation to a just world order. Canadian foreign policy has been, first, the prerogative of the United Kingdom, and is now the prerogative of the United States. In both cases, the primary motivation in foreign affairs has been the consolidation of imperial power. Communitarianism in Canada has always seen ordinary Canadians sympathetic to forms of united nations and international law. But the power of individualism – free enterprise capitalism – has usually placed Canadian governments at the behest of imperial governments of the day.

The forces of communitarianism and individualism are once more locked in combat, this time for internal power in Canada. And this time the attempt is to circumvent the parliament of Canada by the use of a Free Trade Treaty.

But the movement against the supremacy of parliament began before the arrival of the Mulroney Conservatives. Pierre Trudeau's 'patriated' constitution was not merely the result of an action to place amending power in the hands of Canadians rather than people in the United Kingdom. It was a shifting of Canada's system towards U.S. individualism. It was a diminishing of parliamentary power and the recognition of the primary legislative function of corporate capitalism in Canada. And it was the empowering – by appointment rather than election – of a small group of legislators (the members of the Supreme Court of Canada). They represent a very small-selection group closely tied to continental capitalist power. They will respond sensitively and even conscionably to any injustice that does not call continental capitalism into question.

Trudeau made clear that he had open contempt for parliament and for ordinary elected back benchers. He chose, when the occasion arose, to diminish the power of elected members. Quite apart from the fact that the new Charter of Rights is very narrowly conceived, providing, for instance, no rights to unions and no specific rights to native peoples, its structure is undemocratic. The newly empowered Supreme Court might well have mixed elected representatives from the House of Commons with appointees, might have involved elected, representative 'leading citizens' (from Indian bands, women's organizations, unions, etc.) in a revolving process of participation to both democratize and respond to peculiar Canadian needs. But the new empowering of the Supreme Court was a determined narrowing of democratic and communitarian government in Canada, not the opposite.

In their trade unions, their political parties, and in their parliaments, as well as in a number of religious organizations, Canadians have, in the past, successfully maintained some balance between the forces of the dialectic in this country. Again and again, pressures from within legislatures have forced some balance. Now, however, U.S. capitalism in Canada and Canadian capitalism have become increasingly restive with the success of communitarianism in Canada in forcing distribution of wealth. In an October 1986 column for *Report on Business*, Conrad Black, a franker than average Canadian capitalist, put the matter quite simply.

He wants Canada to ape the U.S. with its enormous chasms between wealth and poverty, its position as the most backward industrialized nation in the creation of social insurance safety nets. By having Canada ape the U.S., Black wants to release free enterprise capital in Canada to new freedoms from responsibility. He tells us that Free Trade will solve Canada's problems – as he sees them. In the U.S., he writes,

> Uncompetitive industries have gone to the wall; people have moved to resources instead of the other way round; unionization levels have fallen steeply; strikes are rare and unpopular; taxes lower and simpler.[1]

The way in which Free Trade will create those "benefits" in Canada is to hobble Canadian parliaments and force them to accept U.S. terms of life in Canada – the rule, in fact, of the multi-national corporations. The person who explains how that is to be done is not Black in his column but Madsen Pirie, the man described as the architect of Margaret Thatcher's policy of privatization and deregulation in Britain. His argument for by-passing elected parliaments is made in a book called *Aid By Enterprise* in which he includes an article entitled, "The New Aid Paradigm." Briefly, Pirie's argument is that former methods of providing aid to needy countries have not worked. The new paradigm he advocates has been effective in Hong Kong, Taiwan, Singapore, and South Korea. The governments of those countries are attractive to Pirie. They come nearest to providing an ideal in actively supporting foreign investment, avoiding redistribution of wealth through social insurances, keeping taxes low, advocating free trade, minimizing regulation, permitting open migration, encouraging unhindered mobility of capital, and in providing protection of the properties entrepreneurs accumulate.

The key to the rapacious system Pirie advocates is private property, and he advocates that every precaution be taken to assure the accumulation of private wealth. So determined is he that private wealth is the absolute good that he declares it must be protected "not only from the footpad who comes by night, but also from the majority who come by day in the legislative chamber."[2]

Madsen Pirie recommends, in fact, that powers of government be removed from elected parliaments and placed in the hands of multi-national corporations. That is where Conrad Black appears to be as well, and that is why he believes a Free Trade treaty will remove impediments to unhindered capitalist free enterprise in Canada. Canadian parliaments haven't been inefficient in removing the impediments in the past, as Black seems to believe; they have not wanted to do so, considering many other aspects of life in Canada more important than the unhindered profit of capitalist entrepreneurs. The solution for Madsen Pirie, Conrad Black and other proponents of the New Conservatism is to destroy the powers of elected parliaments.

Clearly, global tides are washing upon Canadian shores. In this country, however, the social record and history are not those of Hong Kong, Taiwan, Singapore, South Korea, the U.S.A., or Britain. In this country the dialectic has had a life of its own.

We have seen some of the bases and working of the dialectic in the preceding pages. We know it is an enduring struggle, and that Canadians often lose in the never-ending battle of opposing forces. To those who forget the conditions of life here, they need only pause a moment to be reminded of some of the painful facts – about the losses. Many forget because of the alienation of Canadians from Canada; many others sustain a monstrous and destructive ignorance of their country.

A highly educated population with a rich history, Canada has virtually no film industry. Three percent of the films shown here are Canadian. In Australia 20 percent of films shown are Australian. In France 49 percent of films shown are French. Canadians don't even distribute film in Canada. U.S. distributors control more than 90 percent of the activity.

Figures like that are mystifying at first glance. But the pattern in Canadian life in this century has been for governments to appeal to the people by practising the rhetoric of self-determination of the culture while quietly assisting in the takeover of all profitable activities. Much is said from both governments and cultural pressure groups about the necessity of maintaining an independent culture, regardless of what happens in the economy. But the two are inseparable. Interests which want to use Canada as a resource base and market view cultural investments exactly as they view any other. Films, videos, books, educational resources, records, discs, magazines, for instance, are highly profitable to those who can control the Canadian market in all aspects. Control has been handed by Canadian government to U.S. interests as the overwhelming policy.

In education 90 percent of text books come from outside Canada – mostly from the U.S.A. Publishing in Canada is a Welfare State operation: Canadian publishers are kept in business simply because their deaths would bare the truth about cultural control. Governments know the truth brutally revealed by the death of a large portion of Canadian publishers would cause an angry public demand for significant change. The present system, therefore, is maintained. It is a system which provides the bulk of profit from the industry to foreign entrepreneurs and provides occasional, uncertain bribes to Canadian publishers (from Canadian tax revenues) to keep them relatively quiet.

Canada's communication minister has recently taken a

leaf from the publishing policy book in order to deal with film in Canada. Years of pressure from filmmakers and information gathered through task forces and other researches have revealed that foreign control of distribution not only strangles the possibility of Canadian-made films being seen in Canadian film houses, it also prevents the development of a healthy Canadian film production enterprise. The Minister of Communications admitted the facts, and prepared legislation to begin to return some power to Canadian distributors as a beginning. U.S. pressure first delayed and then destroyed the legislation. To save face, to present an image of concern, the minister provided legislation that guaranteed control of distribution in Canada to U.S. interests, guaranteed the continued strangulation of the Canadian film industry, but presented several millions of dollars per year for Canadian distributors to compete for distribution interest in some films. The money supplied to 'encourage' Canadian participation comes from Canadian tax revenues. Profits in the film industry will go to U.S. entrepreneurs. Bribes will go to Canadian entrepreneurs.

In both publishing and film the real conflict is clear. By permitting individual enterprise to operate unhindered continentally, advantage has been given to U.S. entrepreneurs because of their size, wealth, and connection to U.S. world power – and because of the susceptibility of the Canadian government to U.S. pressure. The communitarian demand in Canada, however, is tireless – and so has to be silenced. Canadians are not permitted to develop truly effective and dynamic cultural industries, for they would soon control Canadian markets and be ready to compete effectively in the U.S.A. So Canadian government, U.S. government, and U.S. enterprise agree to strangle Canadian cultural institutions.

The number of Canadians in higher education is small enough – and maintained so – to prevent serious leadership on Canadian issues from the universities. Years of struggle against such discrimination resulted some years ago in a half-measure to assure Canadians some fairness of treatment in hiring. A regulation of the Department of Employment and Immigration was put in place to force universities to seek qualified Canadians in Canada before seeking non-Canadians outside of Canada. The regulation was honoured more in the breach than in the observance, but to have some observance was a victory. Recently, an agreement between the Department of Employment and Immigration and the University of Toronto began destruction of the mandatory search for Canadians. Employment and Immigration is preparing to wipe out any assurance that the young, qualified Canadians our universities train will be able to teach in the Canadian university system.

The number of Canadians in symphony orchestras and in positions of policy-making for music in Canada is small enough – and kept so – to assure Canadians will not move significantly towards a strong fabric of Canadian musical culture. The number of Canadian magazines competing with the unhindered dumping of U.S. magazines in Canada is kept small enough to prevent the development of a large, tough, literate, freelance Canadian intellectual group with established audiences.

The National Film Board and the CBC are starved financially as a concerted policy, especially in the areas of creative endeavours and significant coverage of Canadian life – to guarantee a focus away from the Canadian community. That sounds strange. But the genuine development of interest in Canada, as a fundamental need among film and television viewers and radio listeners in Canada, would create a significant force weighing against the establishment of U.S.-style capitalist individualism as the norm and rule for Canadian society. Since its inception in the 1930s, the CBC has been under unrelenting attack by private interests wanting to turn broadcasting into a wholly privately-owned and profit-making operation. Privatization of broadcasting in Canada has been a slow, relentless development in the country over the last 40 years. Governing bodies, eventuating in the present CRTC, have recorded without exerting any penalties regular failures of private broadcasters to fulfill broadcasting requirements of Canadian materials.

Broadcasting in Canada provides a useful model from which to examine the increasing loss of communitarian control of culture. Privatization in Canadian broadcasting – even with tight Canadian ownership rules – means Americanization and an increasingly difficult struggle for Canadian materials to gain access to Canadian media.

In the matter of organized, institutionalized culture and economy in Canada, the anti-communitarian side of the dialectic has achieved and maintained pervasive dominance over the years. The success with which the philosophy of unhindered free enterprise capitalism has been able to effect foreign control and provide policy sympathetic to foreign rule that limits opportunities for Canadians, subverts people working in culture from militant struggle for the Canadian community, and prevents Canadians from being informed about Canada and entertained by Canadians is staggering. The Free Trade Treaty, moreover, will establish that situation as a norm, providing punishment if Canadians attempt to break out of their colonial subjection. According to the treaty, any expansion of Canadian cultural activity in Canada that interferes with present U.S. dominance may be subject to retaliation. The Free Trade Treaty intends to establish the same basis for all profitable activities in Canada, whether cultural, service, industrial, financial, or – eventually – military.

The results of the cultural oppression in Canada – as an example of our general condition – give reason for mixed emotions. Despite the alienation of Canadians from Canada, and despite the alarming ignorance among Canadians about their own country, there is a persistence in a distinct cultural character recognizable among Canadians. The non profit-making culture of Canadian people meeting, talking, running organizations, socializing, observing the world together, planning personal, family, and community futures, operating the workplace, participating in unions, and selecting representative figures other than those presented by bourgeois interests provides a potent force for the continuation of character and identity. Institutional culture is of enormous importance because it provides both a ceremonial recognition of legitimacy and an important organized educational activity. But non-institutional culture has remarkable tenacity, even under the worst conditions.

The dialectic in Canada is a real part of individual personality. Canadians embody both forces. For that reason they have to lose a lot of their right to communitarian existence before they will strike out at individualistic forces. But the case is not completely hopeless, as I have said in speaking of the non profit-making culture of the country. Many national communities with no more reason for survival than Canada have experienced more visible oppression – even extended military occupation – only to re-emerge and re-express themselves, often more certain of identity as a result of the occupying oppressor and a history of quisling collaborators.

No one wants to see his or her country forced into a kind of submergence, a kind of hibernation of identity. But Canadians are very familiar with the experience. Part of their identity, as a matter of fact, is to undergo with equanimity treatment as inferiors in their own land. Terms of the dialectic have dictated the need. On the one hand the outcome can be the cultural fatigue described by Hubert Aquin, which results in surrender and suicide. On the other hand, the result can be a stiffening of resolve, a modification of traditions, and a re-emergence in which all the terms of the dialectic are employed to develop and fulfill the uniqueness of the community's identity.

The Free Trade controversy of the 1980s is the most powerful individualistic thrust of the last part of the twentieth century. Constructed and articulated to destroy the communitarian side of the Canadian dialectic, it intends a massive transformation of Canadian life and Canadian values. Its establishment will engender aspects of the dialectic not before experienced: resistance in new forms; intense debate about the sovereignty of Canadian parliaments; claims by the U.S. to "rights" in Canada; and extremely polarized positions on the desirability and possibility of Canadian survival.

But with or without a Free Trade Treaty the Canadian dialectic will live a dynamic life because the forces that make up its composition have a basis in integrity that has universal relevance. Individualism in all its aspects, as this book has shown, is backed by large historical claims. Communitarianism, equally, can reach into history and theory to establish its legitimacy.

The future, however, rarely takes the shape of theory set out by philosophers or academic thinkers. It is the product of a much more complicated balance and imbalance of forces in contestation and tension. The Canadian identity is blessed and cursed with the character of dialectic, and it is fated to work out its destiny as a moving hand that writes the sentence of our being, a sentence that is never finished and one that will be filled with surprisingly unexpected clauses and interjections.

The nature of our identity requires constant vigilance and constant activity on the part of communitarians to balance the enormous power of individualistic motivation. So far, Canadians have been capable of the necessary energy. Perhaps the nature of our identity should give us reassurance on that score. While we have professed to value individualism and to desire its full flowering, we have often shown ourselves capable of moving as a whole community to secure the dignity and the well-being of Canadians in a way that seriously restrains individualism and articulates a need among Canadians for a balance unique on the North American continent.

Notes

CHAPTER ONE
Opening: The Canadian Dialectic

[1] Canadian Labour Congress, "Surrendering National Sovereignty," in *The Free Trade Papers*, ed. Duncan Cameron (Toronto: Lorimer, 1986), p. 136.

[2] Max Aitken, *Friends* (London: Heinnemann, 1959), p. 75.

[3] F.J. Turner, "The Significance of the Frontier in American History," in *The Turner Thesis*, ed. George R. Taylor (Toronto: D.C. Heath, 1972), p. 5.

[4] F.J. Turner, *The Frontier in American History* (New York: Krieger, 1976), p. 24.

[5] John Dafoe, *Canada: An American Nation* (Columbia University Press, 1935), pp. 11-12.

[6] John Clark Murray, quoted in L. Armour and E. Trott, *The Faces of Reason* (Wilfred Laurier University Press, 1981), p. 123.

CHAPTER TWO
The Conservative Vision

[1] Robert Shuttinger, *The Conservative Tradition in European Thought* (New York: Putnam, 1970), p. 12.

[2] W.L. Morton, "Canadian Conservatism Now," *Contexts of Canada's Past* (Carleton Library, 1980), pp. 243-44.

[3] Ibid., pp. 244-45.

[4] Ibid., p. 246.

[5] Ibid., p. 249.

[6] George Hogan, *The Conservative in Canada* (Toronto: McLelland and Stewart, 1963).

[7] Ibid., pp. 23-35.

[8] Ibid., p. 37.

[9] Ibid., p. 41.

[10] Ibid., pp. 108-9.

[11] George Grant, "Theology and History," in *George Grant in Process*, ed. Larry Schmidt (Toronto: Anansi, 1978), p. 106.

CHAPTER THREE
The Liberal Vision

[1] Hogan, op. cit., p. 31.

[2] Stephen Leacock, *Our Heritage of Liberty*, (New York: Dodd Mead, 1942), pp. 61-62.

[3] Benjamin Ward, *The Ideal Worlds of Economics* (New York: Basic Books, 1979), p. 9.

[4] Ibid., p. 102.

[5] L.T. Hobhouse, *Liberalism* (London: Williams and Norgate, n.d.), p. 47.

[6] A.R.M. Lower, *This Most Famous Stream* (Toronto: Ryerson, 1954), p. 188.

[7] Ibid., pp. 191-92.

[8] W.L. Morton, op. cit., pp. 249-50.

[9] Pierre E. Trudeau, *Federalism and the French Canadians* (New York: St. Martin's Press, 1968), p. 159.

[10] Gad Horowitz, *Canadian Labour in Politics* (Toronto: University of Toronto Press, 1968), p. 16.

[11] Ibid., p. 9.

[12] Ibid., p. 20.

[13] Ibid., p. 21.

CHAPTER FOUR
The Left Vision of Canada

[1] Horowitz, op. cit., pp. 23-27.

[2] Stanley B. Ryerson, *Unequal Union* (Toronto: Progress Books, 1968), p. 424.

[3] Ibid., p. 60.

[4] Ibid., p. 64.

[5] Ibid., p. 36.

[6] Ibid., p. 106.

[7] Herschel Hardin, *A Nation Unaware* (Vancouver: Douglas, 1974), p. 12.

[8] Ibid., p. 54.

[9] Ibid.

[10] Ibid., p. 369.

[11] Richard Allen, "Introduction," in Salem Bland, *The New Christianity* (University of Toronto Press, 1973), p. xiv.

CHAPTER FIVE
Religion in Canada: Its Effect
on Canadian Identity

[1] Quoted in *The Royal Bank Reporter* (Winter 1988): p. 5 (from *Yearbook of American and Canadian Churches*, 1987).

[2] "Religion," *Canadian Encyclopedia* (Hurtig Publishers, 1985), p. 1564.

[3] H.H. Walsh, *The Christian Church in the French Era* (Toronto: Ryerson, 1966), p. 137.

[4] Ibid., pp. 145-48.

[5] Ibid., p. 10.

[6] John S. Moir, "Sectarian Tradition in Canada," in *The Churches and the Canadian Experience*, ed. John W. Grant (Toronto: Ryerson, 1963), p. 125.

[7] Murray G. Ross, *The Y.M.C.A. in Canada* (Toronto: Ryerson, 1951), pp. 37-48.

[8] Sydney E. Ahlstrom, *A Religious History of the American People* (New Haven: Yale University Press, 1972), p. 365.

[9] H.H. Walsh, *The Christian Church in Canada* (Toronto: Ryerson, 956), p. 229.

[10] See for instance Gregory Baum, *Catholics and Canadian Socialism* (Toronto: James Lorimer, 1980); and Gregory Baum and Duncan Cameron, *Ethics and Economics* (Toronto: Lorimer, 1984).

[11] Richard Allen, op. cit., p. viii.

[12] Ibid., p. vii.

[13] A.E. Smith, *All My Life* (Toronto: Progress Books, 1977), pp. 43-44.

CHAPTER SIX
Religion, Economics and Social Structure

[1] Max Weber, *The Protestant Ethic and the Spirit of Capitalism* (New York: Charles Scribner's Sons, 1976), p. 80.

[2] Ibid., p. 175.

[3] Ibid., pp. 181-82.

CHAPTER SEVEN
Quebec and Canadian Identity

[1] Mgr. L.-F.-R. Laflèche, "The Providential Mission of the French Canadians," in *French Canadian Nationalism*, ed. R. Cook (Toronto: MacMillan, 1975), pp. 96-98.

[2] F.X. Garneau, *History of Canada*, trans. Andrew Bell, (Toronto: Belford, 1876), Vol. 1, p. xxix.

[3] Ibid., p. xxxi.

[4] Mgr. L.-A. Pâquet, "A Sermon on the Vocation of the French Race in America," in *French Canadian Nationalism*. ed. R. Cook (Toronto: MacMillan, 1975), p. 154.

[5] Armour and Trott, *The Faces of Reason*, pp. 481-82.

[6] Ibid., p. 488.

[7] Hubert Aquin, "The Cultural Fatigue of French Canada," in *Contemporary Quebec Criticism*, ed. Larry Shouldice (Toronto: University of Toronto Press, 1979), pp. 75-76.

[8] Ibid., p. 78.

Conclusion

[1] Conrad Black, "The Menace Posed by a Yuppie-Ridden Lumpenproletariat," *Report on Business* (October 1986): p. 118.

[2] Madsen Pirie, "The New Aid Paradigm," in *Aid by Enterprise*, eds. E. Butler and M. Pirie (London and Virginia: The Adam Smith Institute, 1984), p. 114.

INDEX